you'll never be 16 again

**an illustrated history
of the british teenager
by peter everett**

BBC Publications

A seven-part series entitled
'You'll never be sixteen again',
produced by Peter Everett, was
broadcast on BBC Radio Four in
1985 and (expanded and revised)
on BBC Radio One in 1986

Design and art direction: Glyn Davies
Cover illustrations: Debbie Cook
Text illustrations: Grahame Baker

To Janey and Felicity,
the teenagers in my life

Published by BBC Publications,
a division of BBC Enterprises Limited,
35 Marylebone High Street,
London W1M 4AA

First published 1986

© Peter Everett 1986
Introduction © John Peel 1986

ISBN O 563 20533 4

Typeset in Univers Light/Baskerville
Colour printed by
Chorley & Pickersgill Limited, Leeds
Typeset, printed and bound in England by
Butler & Tanner Limited,
Frome and London

contents

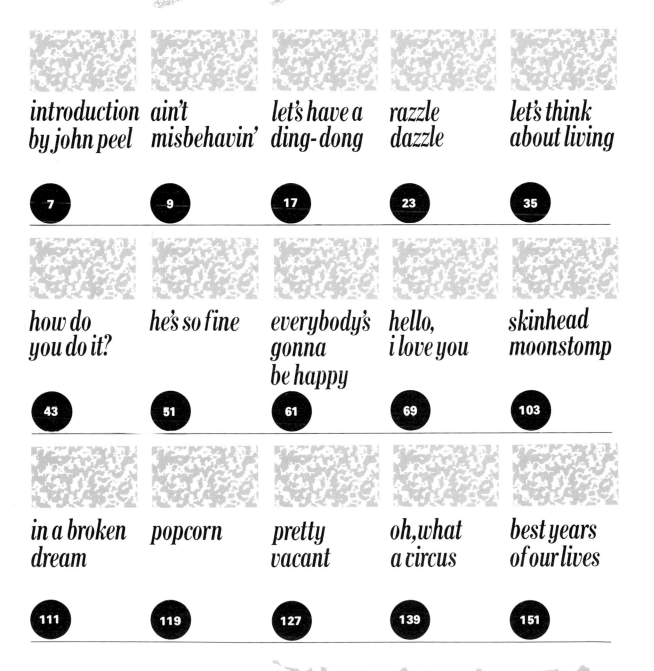

My thanks are due to Michelle Rowland and Julie Simmons, who conducted the interviews quoted in this book and in the radio series on which the book is based.

Thanks also to all those who contributed their thoughts and reminiscences, and to the radio and newspaper journalists from whose work I have quoted. Where possible and appropriate, clearance to quote from published sources has been obtained, for which I am grateful.

In particular, I am indebted to the copyright-holders for their kind permission to include extracts from the following: *Bomb Culture* by Jeff Nuttall (Paladin, 1970); *The Insecure Offenders* by T.R. Fyvel (Chatto & Windus, 1963); *The Boy Looked At Johnny* by Julie Burchill and Tony Parsons (Pluto Press, 1978); *English Life and Leisure* by B.S. Rowntree and G.R. Lavers (Longman, 1951); 'Me', in *The Collected Poems of Adrian Henri* (Allison & Busby, 1986); 'God Save The Queen' (Rotten, Matlock, Cook, Jones), © 1977 Glitterbest Ltd and Warner Bros. Music Ltd.

introduction by john peel

I was sixteen in 1955. The fledgling Peel, then a rather solitary, vacant youth with more hair than was considered entirely *de rigueur*, was serving time at Shrewsbury School. Last year my mother found and gave me my school reports from the period. They do not, I fear, make pretty reading. 'His pose of idleness amuses me but aggravates others,' wrote my form-master. One of the others was more forth-right. 'As beastly as ever,' he began, 'the unpunctuality, inefficiency, inaccuracy, untidiness and idleness are still there. He is no fun to teach.' R.H.J. Brooke, my house-master and a man for whose tolerance and wisdom my admiration grows with every passing year, wrote, 'If he gets a study next term, we want less of Donnie Lonegan and more of the constructive effort.'

The 'Donnie Lonegan' was deliberate. Brooke knew the extent to which my attempts to forge some sort of character for myself, at a school where University still meant Oxford or Cambridge and fail-ure to achieve one or the other led shamed pupils to join the Kenya Rifles or take holy orders, depended on kicking, as it were, against the pricks. My father, perhaps similarly acute, always referred to the King of Skiffle as 'Lollie Dolligan', thereby con-firming me in my admiration for Donegan's nasal Americanisms and apparently anarchic approach to his work.

Trying to explain to listeners less than half my age what life was like for me at sixteen – an explanation, I should hurriedly add, that they rarely seek or welcome – quickly becomes rather like trying to explain cricket to a Frenchman. There were, for example, virtually no gigs to go ▶

introduction

to at all – and they certainly weren't called gigs. The first concert I attended (with my mother) was a performance at the Liverpool Stadium by the Oberkirchen Children's Choir, recorders of one of the most successful versions of 'The Happy Wanderer', an oafish hiking song which had been in the charts for a whole year.

The charts of the period were based on sheet music sales and a successful song – 'Poppa Piccolino' or 'Three Coins in the Fountain', for example – might be available on record in twenty versions or more.

The second live concert I went to – again with my mother – was given by Johnny Ray at the Liverpool Empire. Ray topped a bill which may well, in the spirit of the age, have included comedians, magicians and dog acts. I was rather disappointed with him, as I was a few weeks later with Frankie Laine at the same venue. Laine, whose records I had been buying since hearing a curious work called 'Chow Willy' in the early 1950s, turned out to be a markedly unhandsome man in a suspiciously voluminous suit who could, I noted with horror, have been in his thirties.

This was a time when – or so I believed – women, regardless of age, were attracted only to men in their mid-forties. Nowadays the situation has deteriorated to the point where women, if attracted to men at all, yearn only for those in their late teens and early twenties. This has always struck me as especially unfair.

On the other hand, as a sixteen-year-old my understanding of women, their behaviour and, as it were, geography was virtually nil. I was fourteen before I realised that girls are constructed differently to us chaps. The revelation came whilst playing hide-and-seek ('At fourteen?' I hear you cry) at my godmother's home near Ludlow. I had hidden in the gardener's toilet where I was joined, after some

moments, by a clearly unself-conscious girl of my own age who, to my distress, threw herself onto the Shanks for a pee. I don't believe I can sensibly convey to you my horror at what I saw.

Mind you, even by the standards of the age, I was fairly backward. At school I was so frustrated at my inability to find a soulmate with whom I could discuss the work of Little Richard, Fats Domino and Gene Vincent that in desperation I joined the jazz club, called, with ponderous inevitability, the High Society. I and my newly acquired Earl Bostic record ('Sleep' backed with 'Flamingo' and still worth a listen) were greeted with such condescension by the languid sixth-formers who ran the High Society that I made my excuses and left.

Come to think of it, I have never really found anyone of my own age to share my musical appetites, with the result that when I am dragged protesting to parties in the village where I live, I find myself embroiled in conversations on such lively topics as lagging boilers and stripping pine. I live in hope that one day I will encounter a vet, estate agent or bank manager who is profoundly affected by the Fall or Bogshed.

The impact on my teenage years of hearing Elvis Presley for the first time (on 'Family Favourites') is paralleled by the reactions of those quoted within. The importance of the cheap drain-pipe trousers and hellish green socks I bought in Scotland Road and hid, along with a selection of Health and Efficiencies, in my bedroom cupboard, will become apparent. *You'll Never Be Sixteen Again* helps me to put my own past in order and to realise that I was not, as I thought at the time, stumbling through these experiences alone. For a man who will never be forty-six again, this is somehow obscurely important.

ain't misbehavin'

'I didn't realise I was a teenager, you see. That's the funny thing, you know. There weren't teenagers in those days.'

ain't
misbehavin'

Being a teenager was just something that you got through to be an adult . . . everything good seemed to happen when you were grown up.

Pity the generation that hit puberty at the war's end. They really were 'too old to rock'n'roll, too young to die'. Born into the Depression and evacuated at the outbreak of war, growing up father-less, their lives ruled by the ration book, they had been promised that when the war was over it would all be different.

It wasn't.

In an influential edition of *Picture Post*, published in January 1941, Edward Hulton sketched a picture which remained essentially accurate five years later:

In general, the old are still hanging on to the power and the glory, to the money bags, and to the fun. At places of entertainment they are adequately represented, even upon the dancing floor. At our gay British holiday resorts they seem to constitute 99·9% of the population.

Hulton added an equally prescient word of warning:

The most consistent failure of commonwealths has been to make no use of youth at all. Youth is a force which can be the life-spring of the state. If it is not employed it goes sour, or turns into channels of destructive revolution.

It was the need to employ this life-spring, rather than the need to give it access to power, glory, money and fun, which dictated official policy towards youth in the post-war years. The 1944 Education Act introduced a system of secondary schooling from the age of eleven which would prepare children for their places in the world of work, sepa-rating the artisans from the academics into secondary modern and grammar schools respectively. The supporters of the 'Eleven Plus' examination argued (and still do) that it was the most sens-ible way to ensure that each child would be educated according to his or her abilities.

In practice the Eleven Plus was instantly seen as the sorting of the sheep from the goats. It was as class-based a segregation as that which prevailed in pubs between the saloon bar and the lounge. To pass was to win initiation into the middle class; to fail was to be branded a proletarian.

You were expected to pass your Eleven Plus and go to Grammar School, and if you didn't you were then a failure. You saw your cousins and your friends around you, leaving school at fifteen and going into proper jobs straight away, often things like bank clerks and insurance agents. And this person you knew almost in short trousers would suddenly become a little version of his father. He would be just like him – neat, short-cut hair . . . going and playing golf . . .

In a radio discussion on fashion in 1948, a group of young men mulled over Hardy Amies' opinion that 'The ideal today is that a man should look respect-able and solid without being boring. You want him to look as though he's got a good job and he's going to keep it.' One said: 'The majority of men like to feel that they are wearing something comfortable and not too outstanding. They don't like to look flashy.' Another added: 'The younger males take their fashion from what their fathers wear.' The presenter concluded: 'Well, I think we've all agreed with Mr Amies that we dress to please women, but in a different way from the way women dress to please men. We want to assure them that we have a good job, that we are sound and respectable citizens and that we would make very good fathers of very nice families.'

Whereas the dowdiness of men in those years seemed to some extent a matter of choice, the dowdiness of women was forced upon them. Clothing and textiles were rationed until February 1949, and such garments as were avail-able were plain and skimpily-made. One West End milliner found herself in court for the 'crime' of embroidering roses and butterflies on camiknickers. When their last pair of black market nylons had lad-dered beyond repair, girls stained their legs with gravy browning.

The social lives of the austerity kids were often as threadbare as their clothes:

The only place you could go was a milk bar. We used to go down on a Saturday

morning, and it was very plastic, very shiny, very garish, and there would be nobody else there – perhaps just a couple of down-and-outs. And you would just sit there and drink tea all morning and do nothing else.

The escape from this adolescent limbo was the cinema. It was not uncommon for a young man to take his girl to the pictures four or five times a week. Moreover, it was not necessarily the main feature that was the main feature:

You carried on your courting in the cinema – your kissing and snogging. If you went in the front parlour, you'd still have the family next door. The hallowed room was the front parlour. You could do your courting there, but you'd have the family next door saying 'I wonder what they're doing. I wonder what they're getting up to. Is he kissing her yet?' So your only privacy, the only place you could be together on your own, was snogging on the back row of the pictures.

As for the films they saw when they came up for air, the theme was romantic escape in a dozen different flavours, from pirate swashbucklings to war adventures; gangster shoot-outs to westerns; crinolines to backstage Broadway. For the most part, however, it was an alien, Americanised sort of romance. In short, it was Hollywood. Few of the young cinema-goers felt that what they saw on the screen had much to do with the lives they were leading.

You liked the film stars but I don't think you aspired to be them. You knew it was escapism and you wanted it to be over the top.

I used to love the Fred Astaire films, and all those singing-dancing musicals with very lavish sets and hundreds of dancing girls and transformation scenes.

Hollywood made its mark on British youth in unpredictable ways. In January 1946, the *Daily Mirror* reported:

Children who stay away from school to go tap-dancing are the cause of

the latest headache among education authorities. Rhythm is becoming such a menace to the three Rs that warning was given by one authority yesterday that summonses will be issued against parents whose children are absent from school because they put tap-dancing first.

For every junior hoofer hoping to emulate Astaire, there were a dozen older lads who would leave the cinema practising the Bogart hooded-lid stare, the Cagney swagger or the George Raft trick of flicking a coin across the knuckles.

We used to ape the American movie stars of the time, the gangsters, in particular George Raft. I remember he had a black suit with a fingertip-length jacket and he was always flicking a coin. He was one of my idols. And a lot of us used to buy these suits and sort of pretend to be these stars, and also wear fedora hats – what you'd call the Al Capone hood hat with the snap brim. We must have looked rather silly I suppose, but at the time we thought we looked terrific.

ain't misbehavin'

▼ A tryst outside the Odeon. Some couples went to the pictures four or five times a week.

▼ Hollywood style-setter George Raft with singer Julie Wilson. She's twenty-four but dresses older.

ain't misbehavin'

We had hand-painted ties, which were quite popular at the time. One of the favourites was Jane, the Daily Mirror cartoon – a picture of her, in the nude, hand-painted on red silk.

This was precisely the flashy image which the boys in the radio discussion were at pains to disavow. As the presenter put it, 'You wouldn't want to look like a spiv.' Maybe not, but there were those who would.

The spiv was the first post-war folk-devil. He was a peacetime mutation of the black marketeer, flourishing under austerity like ragwort on a bomb-site. Disliked for jumping the queue, he was tolerated, even smiled at, for his entertainment value and occasionally his usefulness as a source of nylons, whisky or pork chops. In a time of petty bureaucracy gone mad, when the government sought to tell the public not only how much to spend but what it could have for its money, spivs cocked a snook at the system on behalf of all.

The stereotype spiv was a barrow boy in a wide-shouldered, wasp-waisted, baggy-trousered suit of loud pattern (the 'zoot' suit), a dazzling 'kipper' tie, a jaunty trilby and a pencil-line moustache. His style was a model for youthful dress and behaviour every bit as potent as those of the Hollywood tough-guys, the war heroes or the leading sportsmen of the day. In his book *Bomb Culture*, Jeff Nuttall has written of the 'formalised stoicism which we borrowed from the spivs, from demobbed soldiers and from Hollywood movies, which we took and transmuted into a romanticism of toughness and aggression and subsequently wore like a suit of armour'.

Hollywood was not the only American influence on British youth: the US servicemen who had first arrived in 1942 were still coming over to man the bases, charm the ladies and distribute cigarettes and nylons like so many randy Santa Clauses.

They used to organise coachloads of GIs from the bases to local dances. The boys hated them of course, because they had more money and they even smelled nicer. Their uniforms were smarter – polished cotton instead of the rough khaki the Tommies wore. Cuddling an English soldier was like being wrapped in a horse blanket! The Americans brought the girls flowers and boxes of chocolates, and the English boys sneered at them and called them ponces.

To these town and village socials, the GIs brought with them, in a cloud of aftershave, a different way of dancing. 'Jitterbugging' had become popular in the US during the war. It had spread from the black ghettos to dance-halls across the country and was now firmly established in Europe, along with its more formal variant, the jive. They say that, to this day, when they jive in Warrington (down the road from the site of the Burtonwood base) they dance to the off-beat, the way the American hepcats taught their mums forty years ago.

Smart girls took their dance-steps from the 'doughboys', but their fashions came from France. In the spring of 1948, Christian Dior's New Look conquered Britain: the effect was like the simultaneous hatching of a million pupae into a million butterflies, and women still glow when they remember it.

I remember the New Look coming in and that was very, very exciting. Everybody hated it at first. They were so indignant and horrified at the thought that they were going to have these long, full skirts after being free with very short, straight skirts, which was really only to save material during the war. But Dior, I think, knew women better than they knew themselves. He knew that once they got over the shock of it, that's what they were really longing for – those full, feminine, flowing things, lots of petticoats underneath, like a ballerina length really ... Oh that was marvellous! We all wanted those.

▼'One Yank and they're off'. Jukebox manoeuvres, 1952, and the British Army is outflanked by the US Air Force yet again...

I remember having a skirt my mother made out of some curtain material for me, and I thought this was great. People used to say 'Your skirt's made of curtains' and I'd say 'No it isn't!' ...

The first thing was that it was banned at school. We weren't allowed to let down our gymslips or buy long ones.

Underlying all this excitement, there may have been a deeper social current moving women in the direction from which the New Look beckoned.

During the war the women took the men's role. They worked in factories and they ran the home. Then, after the war, they wanted to go back to being pretty, feminine 'little women' again, and being looked after by the men. And perhaps this was sort of encouraged because when the men came back from the war, they wanted their jobs back, so the women had to be sort of pushed back into the home, didn't they?

Although it was worn by girls from fifteen upwards, the New Look was conceived, adapted and marketed for women in their twenties, thirties and forties, the women who always had been, and it seemed always would be, the fashion trade's principal customers.

You tried to look how the models looked, like you saw when you went to the pictures. You tried to emulate the model look – neat, ladylike and sophisticated: two-piece, hat, gloves, stiletto heels, seamed stockings (and the seams had to be straight). If you were sixteen and somebody said you looked nineteen, it was wonderful.

The Hollywood image confirmed it; the great female stars were not *ingénues*, they were mature women in their late twenties or older, sophisticated ladies who knew their way around.

I can remember thinking when I was in my teens, 'Oh, it must be nice to be twenty and sophisticated.' And then when I was in my twenties I thought, 'Well it must be nice to be thirty and sophisticated.' And now I'm fifty and I'm still not sophisticated ...

Although her clothes made her look years older than she actually was, in terms of real sophistication the fifteen-year-old girl of forty years ago was years younger than her present-day equivalent.

We knew absolutely nothing. Nothing at all. I mean, it amazes me that we didn't all get pregnant. Actually, quite a lot of the village girls did have babies, particularly with the Americans.

Sex before marriage was just something that wasn't spoken about. It was all hushed up, like so much in those days. All your mother would say was 'Be careful, whatever you do, or you'll finish up having to get married. You'll ruin your life.'

This enigmatic advice, with its equivalent for boys – 'Don't get a girl into trouble' – did little to dampen youth's perennial interest in the subject.

▼ For sophisticated sipping, white kid gloves were worn with summer frocks.

ain't misbehavin'

All we wanted to know about was sex, because it was so hidden, especially in our school where the girls' half was divided from the boys' half by this mythical barrier. You could see the girls but you couldn't talk to them across the area that was no man's land. There were just a few girls you could talk to, who were 'that sort of girl', you know. Everyone would tell you they were 'that sort of girl' and everybody had done it with them. I mean, I hadn't of course, but everybody else had. That was all we ever talked about. I must admit, quite frankly, that if it had been presented to us we'd have run a mile.

When sexual feelings are repressed, the result is romance, and romance in the late forties and early fifties was a highly marketable commodity. Hollywood, as we've seen, dished it out in vast quantities (as did the women's magazines, which grew in circulation during these years to the point where twelve million British women of sixteen and over were reading two magazines a week) and so did the song-writers and publishers of London's Tin Pan Alley – Denmark St, Soho. The dominant style of popular music was still, as it had been during the war, big band swing. At least, that was what you danced to. For errand boys to whistle, the industry also supplied novelty songs of surpassing silliness, from 'How Much Is That Doggie In The Window?' to 'She Wore Red Feathers And A Hula-Hula Skirt'. And to make the girls swoon, there was the crooner.

Big-time crooning started with Sinatra, who inspired scenes of fan hysteria in the US that had not been encountered there since the death of Rudolph Valentino. Johnny Ray followed, 'the Nabob of Sob', the man who cried all the way to the bank. In an interview during one of his many comebacks, Ray described his effect on British womanhood:

They would smash automobiles and stage doors and everything else. It was not uncommon for little girls to fall down and for other fans to step on them trying to get to me. What amused me more was the press. They were sending psychiatrists into the audience to try to analyse why people were so hysterical; but I imagine at that time I was probably the first performer to go out and lay his emotions right out on his sleeve and just cry to an audience. I imagine they were a little bit shocked and confused about why a grown man would do a thing like that.

The home-grown crooners toured as featured vocalists with the big dance-bands, but Dickie Valentine, Denis Lotis and David Whitfield never had quite the impact of the American originals. Even so, they walked through many adolescent dreams.

It was as though they were singing just to the one girl and ignoring all the hundreds of others in the audience. It was a smoochy, smooth attitude, and sexy if you like. Sexy.

Again it must be emphasised that, like the fashions and the songs, the dance-halls were not primarily for teenagers. Some might have felt themselves too young to be there, but no-one ever felt too old. In 1951, there were 450 Meccas and Locarnos in the UK catering for three million customers a week, as well as thousands of assembly halls and hotel ballrooms licensed for dancing. The typical palais offered dancing six afternoons and evenings a week, with live music, soft drinks and vigilant bouncers, for 1s 6d a session. The authors of *English Life and Leisure* (1951) approved of the ban on alcohol:

Modern ballroom dancing may easily degenerate into a sensuous form of entertainment, and if self-control is weakened with alcohol it is more than likely that it will do so, which might easily lead at least to unruly behaviour and not infrequently to sexual immorality.

They were pleased to note, however, that many dance-halls were now catering for the over-fifties with sessions of 'Old Time' dancing. Some of the halls further obliged their older customers by erecting notices which read 'No jiving permitted', while others conceded a corner of the dance-floor or a portion of the evening to the excesses of the jitterbuggers and the 'be-boppers'.

The young men could afford to be off-hand in their approaches. They were in short supply and could therefore pick and choose their dancing partners. The reason for the shortage of eligible males was National Service.

Since 1960, when conscription was replaced by the hydrogen bomb as the cornerstone of British defence policy, it has often been said that two years' statutory National Service for the country's young men was an excellent thing, teaching them self-discipline, respect for authority and the virtues of hard work. This theory would have been laughed at by many of the lads who were subjected to it at the time. In fact, National Service seems to have had paradoxical effects. For every young man it instructed in discipline, it taught another the value and techniques of 'skiving'. For every promising youngster whose career it impeded, it broadened another's horizons. For every mother's boy it taught to be self-reliant, it reduced another to bed-wetting.

◄ **Humphrey Littleton
fans jive at the
London Jazz Club in
Oxford Street, 1949.**

▼**'Any complaints?'
National Service at
eighteen marked the
end of teenage
freedom for lads like
these. 'All I did was
keep my nose clean
and my head down
and get through it.'**

In the Town Hall in Oxford, the people had a marvellous time. It was just throbbing humanity ... great heat ... great noise. At the end of the dance-floor, by the band, there was a section for jivers, so of course the extroverts used to love to go and perform and we used to stand and watch them, because they were splendid, you know, the men swinging the ladies between their legs and up again, swirling around ...

What appealed to me was seeing twenty-odd musicians all together on a stage, all in uniform, and they played all the latest hits, and you had the singers there as well, and they'd get up. Waltzes, foxtrots, quicksteps, they played all sorts. When that dance-floor was full it was like Old Trafford on a full day, it was absolutely jam-packed.

We used to go as a group of girls together and sit around and wait to be asked to dance, and the boys used to come up and try to be very suave. These young men would sort of look at you and lift an eyebrow and expect you to jump up and dance with them. Or they'd say 'You dancing?' You'd say 'You asking?' ... 'Yes, I'm asking' ... 'OK, I'm dancing.' They must have got it from films I think.

I saw it as an immense waste of time. It was the days when you shaved brush staves. You'd sweep your barracks out with a brush, then you'd actually shave it with a razor-blade to make sure it was still pristine white wood. I have gardened with a dining fork. I'll tell you another one – emptying the coke out of a stove and black-leading the inside of the stove, then putting the coke back in and lighting the fire ...

ain't misbehavin'

There were awful things, like getting a face literally half an inch from yours and a bloke just screaming obscenities at you about how incompetent you are. You've got to stand stock still, not blink and not reply. I found that a bit debasing.

It was tough as far as I was concerned. You know the sort of silly tales they talk about – getting a razor-blade and cleaning the urinals every morning? It happened every morning in Catterick. There were suicides every week. People just couldn't cope. I've seen blokes crying every night in their beds.

But what it did do was teach you a couple of things. One was to be awfully self-sufficient because at the end of this you could iron shirts, you could darn socks, you could sew buttons on, you could clean ... The other was to jump when somebody said jump.

The number of television licence-holders shot up from under 14,000 in 1947 to over 750,000 in 1951. The Coronation in 1953 was seen by more than 20,000,000 people on 2,700,000 sets. By 1957, almost half the adult working-class population was watching 'the box' for an average of four hours every night of the week. It was the beginning of a lasting change in national habits which would do as much as anything to create and sustain teenage culture in the UK. A sixteen-year-old girl, interviewed on the radio in 1958, summed it up like this:

I think it's best to be a teenager now-adays, because most things are for teenagers. I'm dreading to grow old because there's just nothing to do. My mother sits indoors and watches television night after night, and it's getting to be a habit. I'd much rather be a teenager and just go out and provide my own entertainment.

▲ Girls from Kenwood Youth Club gather to watch the first TV show for teenagers, the unmemorable 'Teleclub', October 1953...

▼... But every fifties teenager remembers 'Six-Five Special'. Presenters Pete Murray and Jo Douglas with Lonnie Donegan (centre).

let's have a ding-dong

'You were different because you had your drapes and crêpes and everything. You were unusual. Some people did class you as degenerate but I didn't class myself as that. I used to love it.'

FLICK!

let's have a ding-dong

Towards the end of the forties, while the young men were still sorting themselves into those who would and wouldn't want to look like spivs, a new fashion appeared in the West End of London. It was worn by the young gentlemen about town, the 'debs' delights', who had begun to order from their Savile Row tailors suits cut in the Edwardian manner: long jackets, narrow trousers, velvet collars. They wore them with embroidered waistcoats (such as some of them had acquired to denote membership of the privileged society at Eton known as 'Pop'), curly-brimmed bowler hats and longer-than-usual hairstyles.

What happened next was reported in the *Daily Mirror* in November 1953:

Up and down St James's, heart of the Jeeves country, you may today see furrowed brows under the hard hats of young men about town.

Reason is that the Creepers have pinched the latest fashion of the young men of St James's. And in doing so, they have made it desperately, appallingly unfashionable.

Edwardian suits with high, narrow lapels and drain-pipe trousers, which for some while have been the hallmark of young men at the speakable end of Jermyn Street, are now appearing on Saturday nights from Leicester Square to Hammersmith. With (My dear sir, I assure you!) special hair-cuts.

In fact, the Edwardian style had first crossed the river to Lambeth and the Elephant and Castle some two years earlier. In the process it was exaggerated (jackets got longer, trouser-legs narrower) and embellished. It was given a dash of Wild West gunfighter (string ties, heavy belts), a hint of Hollywood (the 'Tony Curtis' hairstyle) and a couple of other touches of obscure origin, such as fluorescent socks and crêpe-soled 'brothel-creeper' shoes. The result was the Teddy boy.

It is probable that the Edwardian style changed its significance as it spread. Initially a statement of narcissism verging on the theatrical, it then became a uniform for rebels, outlaws or delinquents; in the end it was merely a fashion for any provincial youth who wanted the girls down the Roxy to take him seriously.

In its first and purest form, the Ted style was little more than a way of advertising personal wealth. The whole outfit might easily cost £100 to assemble, and for a lad on about £6 a week that was a lot to accumulate. No wonder the style was so quickly identified with criminality: who could afford to dress that expensively on an honest wage?

A Ted's life was, by later standards, rather boring. He spent his time with his mates, posing on street corners, admiring his reflection in shop windows, or sitting in his local 'caff'. In the early days there wouldn't even be a juke-box, but there might be pinball machines or primitive fruit machines, and a Coca-Cola could be made to last for hours. Once the Teds had moved in, the café was theirs; customers not wearing the uniform were quickly stared out. In effect, the café became the gang's clubhouse.

In an *Observer* article published in June 1955 (by which time Teds had become a national phenomenon, though already dying out in London), Hugh Latimer described the scene well:

In cafés, public houses or milk bars which Teddy boys favour, there is no singing on a Saturday night. The boys sit posed in groups, conscious of arranged hair and creased 'drains', they laugh at the group butt (generally the worst-dressed of the party) and drink intently. Girls sit together waiting to be picked up by somebody

▼ The trousers may need taking in, but the jacket's right, and the pose is immaculate.

and the carrying of an extra long umbrella, which presumably could be used as a weapon. But this feminine intervention was no more than a brief flicker: women's fashions don't arise from below . . .

The more common type of camp followers are rather dumb, passive teenage girls. In my glimpses of them they seemed crudely painted-up, pathetically young, appallingly uneducated, some of them probably in danger of drifting into prostitution – in any case, as I looked at their expressionless faces, I felt sorry for their future families.

◀ **'Rock Around the Clock', 1956: this is how they looked afterwards.**

The Teddy boy gangs, reported a Lambeth youth leader, 'appeared without noticeable standards, except for an almost obsessional loyalty towards each other'. The gangs were indeed tightly-structured. A former Teddy girl from Manchester explains:

You all had your own little groups and them groups made up a big group, and you stayed in that group. You didn't go out with the lads from another group because if you did you'd get a hammering, mostly off the girls, not the lads. The girls would give you a good crack for misbehaving. So you stuck with your own.

It was not until the spring of 1954 that the newspapers began regularly to associate the Teds with outbreaks of violence, directed not so much against ordinary citizens as against other gangs. On 27 April the *Daily Mail* reported:

Cinemas, dance-halls and other places of entertainment in South-East London are closing their doors to youths in 'Edwardian' suits because of gang hooliganism . . .

The ban, which week by week is becoming more generally applied, is believed by the police to be one of the main reasons for the extension of the area in which fights with knuckle-dusters, coshes and similar weapons between bands of teenagers can now be anticipated . . .

In cinemas, seats have been slashed with razors and had dozens of meat skewers stuck into them.

but terribly correct about it all. The picking-up begins with long-distance badinage, both sides remaining seated. Once adopted, girls are a possession to show off, a group possession.

Girls also are the objective of the groups' nightly prowls. A gang in East London is said to be able to call up 150 members within an hour through a system of 'under-governors' to repel groups from other boroughs raiding 'their' women.

The 'creep', a slow spiritless shuffle which now rules the suburban dance-floors, is now so much a favourite of the Edwardians that it can be counted part of the Edwardian personality. It requires little skill and moves only ten yards a minute. Other characteristics are a peculiar dead facial expression, and an enigmatic, monosyllabic way of speech.

The girls got an even worse press than the boys. Here is T. R. Fyvel's description from his influential book *The Insecure Offenders*, published in 1961:

It is worth mentioning that for a brief period a number of girls tried to dress up in conformity with their Teddy boy friends. The recognised style of the Teddy girl included a grotesquely tight skirt, hair worn in a pony-tail,

let's have a ding-dong

The suit, the socks, ▶ the haircut. Newcastle Teds join the overcoat brigade at Club Martinique, 1955.

As well as an early use of the word 'teen-ager' in the British Press, this article also supplies interesting evidence that the slashing of cinema seats by Teds pre-dates the arrival of *Rock Around the Clock.*

Much was made of the Edwardians' alleged fondness for flick-knives, razors and bicycle chains. There was talk of their sewing fish-hooks behind their lapels so that an aggressor, seeking to get a grip in readiness for a 'nutting', would lacerate his fingers; but it seems doubtful that lethal weapons were used in earnest on a wide scale. They were essentially props for posing with: most first-hand accounts of gang battles insist that the preferred weapons were sticks, stones, bottles and boots. After all, nobody wanted to hang, so the aggression was ritualised:

Fights were pre-arranged, they didn't just happen. One leader would say to another 'Right, we'll meet you at such-and-such a place, Saturday night, eight o'clock, have a fight.' So if you wanted, you'd all amble down there. There'd be one side, you know, booing and cheering, the other side booing and cheering. And you know, it was fight, fight, fight and then we all went back: they went back to their place and

we went back to our place. And you know, that side had won that week; a couple of weeks afterwards we'd win. So it was pre-arranged: 'You'll win this week, I'll win next week', I'm sure.

Sociologists in the fifties had not yet developed the theory of 'deviancy amplification', but the Teddy boy panic that possessed newspapers and watch committees over the next couple of years provides a classic example of the process in action. Simply stated, the theory proposes that when a group is defined by society as 'deviant', it acknowledges the definition by exaggerating its outlaw behaviour. Meanwhile, those members of the group who prefer not to be so drastically stigmatised drop out, leaving the hard core, who then gather new recruits for whom the deviant image is the attraction.

The figures for juvenile crimes of violence bear out the theory. From 1950 to 1955 they dropped year by year. Then, after the newspaper hysteria erupted, the figures rose again, year by year, through the rest of the decade. Dr Josephine Macalister Brew, writing in 1957, probably got it right when she said: 'The relatively few cases of unquestionably violent gang behaviour

let's have
a ding-dong

have been magnified out of all proportion to their incidence.' First-hand accounts of Ted violence bear this out:

I remember a band being booked at Chatham Town Hall, and I did get into a bit of a kerfuffle with the sax player who wouldn't play 'Rudy's Rock' or something that I wanted him to play. In the end I remember kicking his saxophone and being done for wilful damage to a saxophone. I mean, that's what the policeman put on his note at the time. I was fined £2.

The Teddy boys would come down to Weston-super-Mare. I don't think they were coming down looking for a fight or anything, because there was no-one else to fight. But the police wouldn't let them off the station approach. They'd all pour down when the three trains from Bristol would arrive in half an hour, and 500 Teddy boys would get off and they'd be stuck in the station approach and obviously they got grumpy. They'd be milling about because they wanted to go on the pier and go on the dodgems, and there were all these police herding them around and forcing them back on the trains again, and British Railways wouldn't want them back because they were a load of grumpy Teddy boys who were even more grumpy now and they would obviously rip the train to shreds, so there'd be 500 Teds stamping about, and occasionally windows got broken because of the sheer pressure of crowds. But the ones I knew always seemed perfectly reasonable people. They never got much real damage done.

Ordinary people, the working-class people, they quite approved of them. I mean, there wasn't nearly the violence then that there is now. I mean, you would see two Teddy boys carrying home their mother's shopping.

None of this was news, of course. News was violence, or at least the establishment response to a perceived threat of violence. 'WAR ON THE TEDDY BOYS', screamed the *Sunday Dispatch* in June 1955. 'MENACE IN THE STREETS OF BRITAIN'S CITIES IS BEING CLEANED UP AT LAST'.

At Liverpool, vigilantes are watching for Teddy girls. They wear jeans, shirts and 'jelly-bag' hats and carry knuckle-dusters and bicycle chains.

Policewomen in tight skirts and 'sloppy-Joe' shoes (sic) mingle with dance-hall and cinema crowds to watch for trouble.

Policemen run a 'Teddy boy squad' of radio-controlled Land Rovers with police dogs aboard...

At some cinemas, security guards who are ex-Commandos and professional boxers are mounted on all doors, and barbed wire has been put up to keep out the gangs.

Respectable patrons were presumably issued with wire-cutters. A week earlier, Hugh Latimer's *Observer* article had reported:

Youthful experts in South London insist that the Teddy suit is out, finished, that in six months time there will be none to be seen on the streets, unless used for going to work.

Edwardianism's short-lived popularity in London is blamed on a bad press and a hostile public opinion. Only social workers, tailors, barbers and intellectuals have a good word for Teddy boys, and they themselves use the word pejoratively. Cinemas, milk bars, public houses and cafés are being closed to them, mothers try to stop their daughters going out with them, men ridicule the dress as effeminate.

The Teds were never more than a small minority of their age-group. Most teenagers felt the influence of their style, shuddered at tales of their evil-doing and were fascinated by their seedy glamour, but always at second-hand.

There was nothing there until the Teddy boys came along, and then you looked at them and thought 'I must do something myself', but if my mother had seen me in the full Teddy boy outfit, she would have gone berserk. So you did the half-hearted thing – perhaps the suede shoes, possibly the fluorescent socks, took in the trousers

let's have a ding-dong

(that upset mums a lot I think) . . . It was half a quiff, no sideboards. I used to actually blacken my cheeks with burnt cork to go to choir practice, to pretend I had sideboards . . . Fake, not-quite-right hair . . . a long jacket, but not a proper drape jacket . . . a narrow tie but not the narrowness that they had, not the string tie . . . But you could never do the full thing, you know, the thing that they did, if you were not a true Teddy boy. I mean, you just did half. It was always half-way.

In 1961, T. R. Fyvel interviewed a young man who had belonged to a Teddy boy gang before his National Service in the Navy, and asked him what had happened to the original Teds:

Some were put away. Borstal, quite a lot went to. What happened to most of the others was exactly what happened to ordinary people in ordinary life – mixing with the opposite sex and sooner or later they'd go steady and they'd end up pushing a pram.

**Dover Barracks, 1956. ▶
This hairstyle has
only minutes left
to live.**

razzle dazzle

'Elvis Presley, "Heartbreak Hotel"!
... You just thought, "What is
that?" It was incredibly exciting,
incredibly rebellious, and you just
thought, "That's it. THAT IS IT!
I dedicate the rest of my life to
whatever that is!"'

razzle dazzle

Rock'n'roll was a consequence of the limited racial desegregation in the US which had followed the war. Until the early fifties, black entertainers were accepted in 'showbiz' if they mocked their race (Amos 'n' Andy, Bert Williams), or if their talent was, by white cultural standards, outstanding (Paul Robeson, the Inkspots). On the black side of the great divide, however, there was a tradition of music which had evolved out of jazz, gospel and blues to meet the needs of an exclusively black audience. By the late forties it was recognisably something else; in fact it was several somethings else: boogie-woogie, jump blues, second-line, doo-wop and a dozen other styles, some pure, some hybrid, all black. There had been musical cross-fertilisation across the black-white barrier, but it had been the musicians' secret. It hadn't had the effect of mixing up the audiences.

When white teenagers in the US became consciously separate from their parents on the one hand and their kid brothers and sisters on the other (an awareness that occurred earlier there than in the UK), some of them began to tune their radios to black stations and listen to this stuff, in spite (or probably because) of the fact that their parents regarded it as 'jungle music'.

The new market did not go unnoticed. A Cleveland disc-jockey called Alan Freed was probably the first broadcaster to play black records for a white audience and he claimed to have coined the term 'rock'n'roll' to describe what he would otherwise have had to call 'race music'. The audience grew, and before long, white musicians latched onto the sound and began to reproduce it in a deodorised form.

With the exception of the few who took a specialist interest in obscure American records or tuned their radios to AFN (the American Forces Network), British teenagers were unaware of rock'n'roll during its formative years. The beast therefore leapt the Atlantic full-grown and ravening, and its impact was all the greater for the delay.

There had been straws in the wind. In September 1955, South London cinemas had reported Teddy boy disturbances at showings of *The Blackboard Jungle*, which featured a brief appearance by Bill Haley singing 'Rock Around The Clock'. But it was almost a year before the film-of-the-song-from-the-film opened in Britain and rock'n'roll became a matter of national controversy.

I'd read in the paper that there was this film and kids were tearing up the cinemas, so I went to the cinema and, sure enough, as soon as it started off, with one accord the audience leapt to its feet and started bopping about in a way I'd never seen before in my life. I was looking at the screen and then the audience as if I'd been at Wimbledon. I was totally bowled over by the simple display of animal force and energy, and I loved it.

I went three times to see that film. Then we'd be dancing coming home, in the middle of the road with all our friends, remembering the footsteps and everything.

On 10 September 1956, the *Manchester Guardian* described the scene at the Odeon thus:

The film was stopped for eighteen minutes, in the hope that the uproar among the audience of 900 would subside, but each time one of the 'rock and roll' bands interrupted the story of the film with the first manic whine of a saxophone, boys leapt from the front stalls into the front aisle and stamped their suede shoes in the octopus whirling of jive.

Young people at the back of the cinema, when they were not training fire-hoses, gave vent to their emotion by stretching their arms out to the screen like savages drunk with coconut wine at a tribal sacrifice. Sometimes they flung their lighted cigarettes about: always they chanted the

▼ Rudi Pompelli, the Comets' sax-man, punishes the bass-player for turning up with odd socks. Bill Haley is the comparative youngster with the kiss-curl.

songs and banged out the insistent beat on the carpet. Even two usherettes were seen tapping their hands against the chocolate trays.

Two days later, the rioting spread to the streets. *The Times* kept track of the damage:

Two policemen were injured when police were called to disperse a crowd singing and 'jiving' in the New Kent Road, near the Elephant and Castle, London, late last night after a performance of the film *Rock Around The Clock* at the Trocadero cinema. Bottles and fireworks were thrown and four shop windows were smashed.

Watch committees in other towns and cities moved quickly to ban the film. It was debated by eminent panelists on 'Any Questions'; Lord Boothby declared that 'one of the purposes of us old fogies in life is to stop young people being silly.' Jeremy Thorpe MP called the film 'musical Mau Mau' and said he was worried that 'a fourth-rate film with fifth-rate music can pierce through the thin shell of civilisation and turn people into wild dervishes'.

The Bishop of Woolwich wrote to *The Times* supporting the idea of a ban. He was worried about 'a steady growth of jive':

The hypnotic rhythm and the wild gestures have a maddening effect on a rhythm-loving age-group and the result of its impact is the relaxing of all self-control.

The hysteria soon cooled and rock'n'roll became a youthful foible to be greeted with an indulgent smile. In December 1956, when a group of people yelled 'See you later, alligator' to the Duke of Edinburgh as he boarded the Royal Yacht *Britannia* in Port Lyttleton, New Zealand, he shouted back 'In a while, crocodile' and, according to the *Daily Telegraph,* 'young people in the crowd howled their delight'.

By the time the next big rock'n'roll movie, *The Girl Can't Help It,* arrived the following year, the royal family's hepcat credentials were impeccable. Princess

Margaret not only went to see the film, she was reported to have actually tapped her stockinged feet on the brass rail of the Royal Circle.

Meanwhile Haley himself had come and gone. His UK tour in February 1957 effectively burst the bubble. Promoter Tony Hall, who hated the music anyway, was gratified to note that:

When the kids saw what he looked like – an old man with a kiss-curl and a band full of even older men in plaid jackets, lying on the floor playing double basses under their chins – it was just terrifying, it really was. Ironically, they never sold any records at all. You couldn't give them away after they'd been here.

Fortunately, other American rock'n'-rollers were on their way. In the meantime, Tin Pan Alley, still wedded to the supremacy of Moon, June and David Whitfield, was fighting off a guerrilla movement: skiffle.

Lonnie Donegan arrived in the Top Ten in January 1956 with three great advantages over his competitors. First, although he sounded American, he was British; this helped him survive the first wave of imported rock'n'roll. Second, although he was British, he sounded American; this made him fashionable. Third, any British youngster who could afford five shillings' deposit for a guitar could hope to sound like Donegan inside a fortnight.

Skiffle was black American folk-song of pre-war vintage, set to a shuffle rhythm supplied by such improvised instruments as washboard, tea-chest bass, seven gallon jug (which, blown correctly, makes a wonderful farting noise but which never caught on in the British revival) and even comb-and-paper. Ken Colyer's Jazz Band featured interludes of skiffle in performances during the early fifties, and Donegan, who had joined in these sessions, put a couple of the songs onto a Chris Barber LP. One in particular, 'Rock Island Line', was requested so often on the radio that it was released as a single furnishing the first of twenty-six Donegan hits and starting a craze.

I was in a skiffle group. We used to have red shirts and black jeans. We were called the Blackjacks. I could play one doo-dah on the guitar, and that was D7. That

▲ Washboard, guitar, kazoo and broomstick-bass ... the City Ramblers Skiffle Group keep it simple.

It's unlikely that the ▶ fans were screaming at the sweater, but the way Elvis moved was something else.

with two Bill Haley songs and a Fats Domino classic ('Ain't That A Shame' in its bleached Pat Boone version) among the best-sellers. Although it ended with Johnny Ray and Guy Mitchell still dominating the 'hit parade', further down the list, things were changing. Little Richard was at number five with 'Rip It Up', and Elvis Presley, who had first appeared in May with 'Heartbreak Hotel', was now enjoying his seventh British hit. Even *The Times* had heard of him; in September 1956 it told its readers of:

... a raw young Southerner, Mr Elvis Presley, now only twenty-one, whose combination of a hill-billy style of wailing with bodily contortions that are supposed to suggest the 'fundamental human drive' took him even beyond the peaks of popularity enjoyed most recently by the tearful Mr Johnny Ray and Mr Frank Sinatra.

His records, notably such items as 'Heartbreak Hotel' and 'Hound Dogs' (sic), have sold something in the region of ten million copies, and, whatever his erotic appeal, Mr Presley has become a national craze.

meant three fingers, and all the time on D7 I was just strumming away, and I thought that was terrific!

In '56 it was a guitar! They were things that they had in the window at Woolies and they were £6 19s 6d. It was your wildest dream until you got it home and you started to press down those three strings to make A. Goodness me, I remember it actually shredding your fingers. What do you expect with a guitar that cost £6 19s 6d?

The skifflers who persisted and progressed went in two directions. Some acquired primitive amplifiers, electric guitars and drums and mutated into rock'n'roll groups along the lines of Cliff Richard and the Shadows or Buddy Holly and the Crickets. Others retreated into the insulated world of the folk clubs, where electricity was a dirty word and the perennial topic of conversation was 'Can white men sing the blues?'

To the purists, skiffle and rock'n'roll are entirely different kinds of music, but to the teenagers it was all the same thing: it was rhythm, drive and excitement, it came from the US, it made you want to jig about and it was for you, not your parents.

1956 was the pivotal year for rock'n'roll in the UK. The year began

I was a great Elvis Presley fan from the word go. I bought every 78, every 45, every LP. I could not get enough of Elvis Presley. For me it was the dancing; he was just unbelievable, and I think that male and female alike were impressed by that. It wasn't a case of 'All the girls loved Elvis Presley.' I remember lots of males being just as impressed.

... And when I first saw Little Richard, I was completely knocked out. I knew he was black, but I didn't know he looked the part: the baggy trousers, the long jacket, and jumping up on his piano and the four big black tenor sax players booting out the solos in the background ... I mean that's what rock'n'roll's all about.

The first time I heard Little Richard I thought 'Christ, you know, how is this not illegal, to get this much sex, energy, drive and violence onto a piece of plastic?'

The fact that it *was* plastic was significant. The replacement of the heavy, breakable 78 by the 45 r.p.m. 'single' was one of the technical developments that helped the first wave of teenage music to form. Now you could take a couple of dozen discs to the youth club without spraining your shoulder.

At around the same time the valve-powered record-player replaced the wind-up gramophone; the 'Dansette' was portable and it had an 'autochange' device which allowed you to play a stack of records one after another (or to set the same record to play time and time again). Technology plus economics, as well as the new kind of music, helped to push record sales from £3.5 million in 1950 to £15 million by the end of the decade.

Then came the 'tranny'. Radios became smaller and cheaper, until for £10 or so you could buy a little plastic pal that played Radio Luxembourg under the bedclothes. Parents who heard their children speak of the 'Under The Bedclothes Club' launched by Jimmy Savile on Radio Luxembourg must have wondered what was going on. Conversely juke-boxes and record-playing equipment in clubs and dance-halls got bigger and louder. The new amplification equipment for groups made it possible for four or five lads to make more noise than a full-scale dance-band. It was also portable, especially after the electric bass guitar replaced the cumbersome acoustic double bass. The technology that would help to create the beat boom of the early sixties was gradually assembling itself. The first dance-hall disc-jockeys were appearing, the ubiquitous Savile prominent among them. The Palais gave up the unequal struggle and allowed the jivers to take over.

We went to Chorlton Palais: it was Monday; Tuesday; Wednesday (Thursday I had to stay in and wash my hair and have a bath); Friday; Saturday dinner; Saturday night; Sunday dinner, Sunday night. And then there was the Plaza in town, dinner-time jiving, so we went there an' all. You didn't do anything else, you just jived all the time.

Everybody was throwing everybody under their legs and over their shoulders ... I used to go to the Plaza every dinner-time. It cost us sixpence for two hours. The thousands that used to go there! They had it on from twelve till two, and I only had an hour for my dinner. I used to sneak the two hours and creep into work so that nobody would see me. But I wasn't on my own – everybody else was doing the same, and of course at that time you could walk in a job and get sacked, then go and get another job in the afternoon. It was that easy to go and get jobs.

As 1956 rocked on, it became clear to the music moguls that the established roster of British singing stars was not equal to the job of covering the American rock'n'roll hits. Michael Holliday was never going to do a convincing 'Hound Dog'; Frankie Vaughan might get away with 'Green Door' but he wasn't quite up (or down) to 'Long Tall Sally'. What was needed was a British Elvis. His arrival was announced in the *Daily Mirror* in September in precisely those terms:

'Presley? I hate him!' said the boy who looks like becoming the first of Britain's Elvis Presleys ... a slim, blond-fringed bundle of energy named Tommy Steele from the same dockside parish of Bermondsey as Max Bygraves.

razzle dazzle

A few weeks ago, Tommy, nineteen, was a merchant seaman. Now he gets a recording and cabaret break after being 'discovered' singing rock'n'roll in a London coffee house.

My verdict: Tommy can help himself to some of the rock'n'roll gravy. He's bright, 'lively', infectious. What's more, you can understand most of his words.

Steele's first record was not, as it turned out, a cover version. With the arrogance of ignorance, his promoters imagined that anything American songwriters could do, Lionel Bart could do better. The result was 'Rock With The Caveman', which got to number thirteen and the moguls thought again. For their second attempt they gave the lad a Guy Mitchell swingalong number 'Singing The Blues', and this time they were in rock'n'roll gravy up to their ears. Mitchell's version went to number one, but Tommy's was at number two; the following week the records changed places and within six months of the lad's launch into show business they were filming *The Tommy Steele Story*.

You had to go to the record shop and queue for four Saturdays in a row to get your copy of 'Singing The Blues'. I mean, he was the number one British person. If we went to family parties, every cousin would get up and imitate Tommy Steele.

▼ **Cliff Richard and his 'Summer Holiday' pals pointed the way to continental frolics for a more adventurous sixties generation of young holiday-makers.**

I remember he was in blue and he had silver stripes up his leg. You couldn't hear a word he was singing 'cause everyone was screaming. They turned the fire-hoses on us to clear the street, and I had no voice for about two days afterwards.

Colin MacInnes wrote: 'He is Pan, he is Puck, he is every nice young girl's boy, every kid's favourite older brother, every mother's cherished adolescent son.'

In other words, Tommy was not the British Elvis at all. He presented about as much of a challenge to the establishment as an Ealing comedy. It soon became apparent that he was indeed from the same parish as Max Bygraves, with 'a handful of songs to sing you', one of which was about a little white bull whose mummy wouldn't let him go to the bullfight. But for a while the teenagers loved him because he was all they had.

The British Elvis (Mark Two) was another ex-skiffler, but this one was launched into a more precise trajectory. As Cliff Richard himself later acknowledged:

The climate was absolutely perfect for someone like me to come in and be the Elvis of Great Britain; not that I personally wanted to be, although I was totally influenced by him originally, you know, but there it was: there was this gap and I filled it.

The result was reviewed by 'The Alley Cat' in the *New Musical Express:*

This columnist has always high praise for the 'Oh Boy!' television series. But producer Jack Good must be held responsible for permitting the most crude exhibitionism ever seen on British television by Cliff Richard last Saturday.

His violent hip-swinging during an obvious attempt to copy Elvis Presley was revolting – hardly the kind of performance any parent would wish their children to witness.

The aspects of Elvis's image that came most easily to Cliff, however, were the modesty, the earnestness, the respectability and the deference to authority which Presley projected whenever he was interviewed. In that respect Cliff left his mentor at the starting-post, as he proved during a 1962 radio interview:

The teenagers I meet are perfectly normal, but the odd ones that scream ... people say 'Look at that screaming teenager', and immediately

you've got the generalisation again, you know, and I think that we're all fighting against this, and I feel embarrassed and disappointed sometimes.

I'd just like to say that I hope people don't take what we sing too seriously, and if we say anything in the Press, I hope it's the right thing. But it's so difficult because what I feel is right may not be, you know? And I hope to be told, so I hope everyone else wants to be told.

As an apology for wiggling his hips a little, this was positively fulsome, but it was about as rebellious as British rock'n'roll ever became. The Larry Parnes 'stable' of ersatz Presleys that followed – Marty Wilde, Billy Fury, Vince Eager, Dutty Power and the rest – did precious little to live up to their dime-novel names. Adam Faith, for example, seemed quite overwhelmed by the responsibility of being chosen as a spokesman for British youth. He was interviewed on 'Face to Face', introduced on television to the Archbishop of Canterbury and questioned about teenage morals by the British Medical Association. He said the quality he most wanted to be admired for was sincerity.

As for Tommy Steele, he said:

I always keep to a certain motto: do what you dig, dig what you do, and in all you dig and all you do, live up to the name teenager.

The teenager-as-consumer took fourteen years to cross the Atlantic. In 1945 a Chicago student called Eugene Gilbert set up 'Gil-Bert Teen Age Services', a specialist marketing company which made a lot of money in the US. By 1956 he was ready to open a London office, but it closed within a year because he judged that British teenagers 'haven't enough freedom or enough money to be commercially interesting'. This was clearly a misjudgement, based on the fact that British manufacturers and retailers were simply not interested in the youth market. They stayed out of it because they didn't understand it, and left a vacuum to be filled by American music, continental clothes, French films and Italian scooters. Meanwhile the post-war baby-boom was moving through the population, and by 1959

◄ The US teen dream in its purest form: Ann-Margret and Bobby Rydell.

there were five million British teenagers with money to spend. That was the year that realisation dawned, with the publication of Mark Abrams' pamphlet *The Teenage Consumer*, which marshalled the available statistics to make some startling points:

After he has met his fiscal obligations to the State and to his parents, the average young man is left with about £5 a week to spend as he chooses ... the average young woman is left with about £3 ...

Abrams estimated that, including pocket money and extending the definition of 'teenager' to include unmarried people under twenty-five, there was available 'a grand total of £900 millions a year to be spent by teenagers at their own discretion'. This was, *in real terms,* twice the pre-war figure.

So what did they buy? Abrams' answer, which now seems obvious, was then something of a revelation. They spent their money on clothes, shoes, drinks and cigarettes, on snacks and cups of coffee in cafés, on pop records and gramophones to play them on, on magazines, on going to the pictures and on going dancing. 'In other words', he concluded, 'this is distinctive teenage spending for distinctive teenage ends in a distinctive teenage world.' (As an advertising man, Abrams clearly knew the value of repetition.)

There was one more fact of crucial importance, and it separated teenagers

*razzle
dazzle*

from adults as dramatically as the Berlin Wall separates East from West: teenagers from poor homes were rich; teenagers from rich homes were poor. Abrams put it like this:

The teenage market is almost entirely working-class; its middle-class members are either still at school or college or else just beginning on their careers; in either case they dispose of much smaller incomes than their working-class contemporaries and it is highly probable, therefore, that not far short of 90% of all teenage spending is conditioned by working-class taste and values. The aesthetic of the teenage market is essentially a working-class aesthetic.

Abrams' message was received with rapture by retailers and with horror by headmasters. 'With new teenagers arriving at the rate of half a million a year', the *Draper's Record* pointed out, 'the teenage trade cannot be treated as a sideline.' 'Miss Norvic Teenager' was crowned to celebrate the fact that the average teenage girl bought twice the average number of shoes.

By the turn of the decade, Abrams' revelation had become conventional wisdom. *The Observer* reported on New Year's Day, 1961:

In the opinion of headmasters, youth is 'a piece of cake' for commercial exploiters, whose witchcraft has transformed the pre-war adolescent into the post-war teenager. In their report, which is to be considered at the conference of the Association of Headmasters in Nottingham this week, they say that the word 'teenager' … has been remorselessly promulgated – plugged, in fact – by the skilled exploiters of the media of mass advertisement: the popular Press, the cinema, radio, television, and the million-reader magazines, for whom the teenager now represents the consumer group with the highest proportion of 'loose' money to spend.

From such spell-binders the teenagers can only learn that happiness has little to do with self-control or the Sermon on the Mount, and much to do with being glamorous, rich, attractive to the other sex, the lucky winner, and all such stuff as adolescent dreams are made of.

That definition of teenage happiness has a certain period charm when set alongside the 'sex and drugs and rock'n'roll' formula of a decade later, but in 1961 sex wasn't discussed, drugs hadn't arrived, and rock'n'roll was finished.

The difference between 1955 and 1958 can be measured in many ways: it is the difference between 'Stranger in Paradise' and 'Great Balls of Fire'; between *Separate Tables* and *A Taste of Honey*; between the Bluebird Café and the Mogambo Coffee Bar.

The latter divide was wider than the mere shift from tea-for-two to cappuccino. The continental coffee bar was

The telephone at ▶ home was a fifties status-symbol that meant a lot to teenagers.

◄The coffee bar was a place to talk. Frothy cappuccino was served in transparent plastic cups, and you sipped it slowly to make it last.

taking over from the drab egg-on-toast 'caff' with its steaming urns and its tin ashtrays; it was also replacing the clattering tea-shop – the Lyons or Kardomah, where permed ladies kept their coats on and nibbled fancy cakes – and it was a welcome alternative to the pub as a place to sit and chat.

As a girl, you didn't really go anywhere on your own. Two girls wouldn't have gone into a pub and sat there by themselves. It would not have been worth their while. They would have been tarts and that's it.

No, girls couldn't go in pubs, and when the coffee bars came out it was an absolutely heaven-sent opportunity. I mean, it must have been a total emancipation for those fifteen- or sixteen-year-old girls to be able to go out and sit for the evening and sip coffee and see fellas.

It seems instantaneous now. One minute there were none, and then there was perhaps one, and that one became so popular that there would be hundreds of people outside on the pavement waiting to get in. The juke-box would be in the cellar and there would be this thump coming through the pavement, and you were quite happy to mill about outside, with several hundred other people, just for the chance to get in there and sip not-very-good coffee for ten minutes and then be shoved out again. But then, very rapidly, lots more opened, and then they divided up into places for various types of people. There were very sophisticated ones above a department store, then real rock'n'roll ones, ones for foreign students and ones for beatniks.

Illustrated Magazine, in March 1958, was nervous of the coffee bar phenomenon. It quoted a probation officer:

Young men and women today crave for bright lights – or no lights at all. They sit in coffee bars, some of which are dark, unhealthy dungeons; dens that are breeding grounds for juvenile crime.

There were now 3000 coffee bars, the magazine claimed, and the 'Espresso Boom' showed no signs of diminishing.

Today the teenager has money to spend. The cheerless parish hall, the wooden youth hut, leave him cold. Rightly or wrongly . . . the craving is for luxury, atmosphere, music and glamour, which means attractive girls. The coffee bars, with their candle-light, Mexican masks, bamboo decor and beautiful waitresses, have certainly found a gimmick to appeal to the young.

That was laying it on a bit thick, but the article was quite right to observe that the coffee bar was part of the process by which teenagers were creating a social world for themselves, away from adult supervision or interference. They had not yet articulated an identifiable philosophy beyond cheerful hedonism. Their concerns were largely restricted to clothes and music, but these topics alone were sufficiently controversial to make 'the generation gap' a very hackneyed phrase in a very short time.

razzle dazzle

We began the revolting. I'm sure we did begin the revolting. I mean, I remember teenage as one constant niggling battle to push back yet another frontier, to be allowed just one more item of clothing or silly hair-style that your parents were still trying to claw back . . . terrible struggles to try and get you to go out of the house looking presentable. And the hair-dos! The hours you spent in front of the mirror, back-combing, raking a comb through so that your hair stood on end and then you had to sort of mould it into a huge beehive on top, so that it was miles above and to the side of your head.

The winklepickers! Those were the first shoes that I really fought and struggled for. A pair of white winklepickers with very pointed toes and little pointed heels . . .

We worried about enjoying ourselves and what we were going to wear on Saturday night and who we were going to go with. We were completely selfish. Nothing occurred to me. I lived in a little self-indulgent world. I'd ring up a friend and we'd meet Saturday afternoon and we'd go to the shops and listen to fifty records and buy one and have our hair done and come home and expect food and then go out again. But the sort of friction would be that I was indolent, lazy, that I lay around on the floor listening to complete junk on my record-player and didn't do a thing. That caused the friction.

▼ **Jay Kinney's cover for a seventies fanzine captures a bad moment in teenage history: February 3rd, 1959.**

Those in charge of radio and television had no more idea than any other adults how to cope with these fretful adolescents. Teenage musical tastes were not catered for in the day-to-day output of the Light Programme, which had been accustomed to sort its audience into children, workers and housewives and to give them programmes called 'Children's Favourites', 'Workers' Playtime' and 'Housewives' Choice'.

Skiffle did find a thimble-hold on a Saturday morning in a programme entitled, with typical Light Programme imaginativeness, 'Skiffle Club'. As thimble gave way to plectrum and we entered what many now remember as 'the Bert Weedon years', the name changed to 'Saturday Club'. In due course a Sunday morning version was added, which the producers in a fit of anarchism called not 'Sunday Club' but 'Easy Beat'.

Restricted by the BBC's contract with the Musicians' Union to a niggardly ration of needletime, these programmes relied heavily on resident musicians and singers chosen less for their individual brilliance than for their willingness to have a bash at anything from 'High School Confidential' to 'Sing Little Birdie'.

Television was equally tentative, and 'Six-Five Special' was presented by Pete Murray, Jo Douglas and the boxer Freddie Mills in the embarrassed style of a youth-club leader kicking off a bit of a sing-song. Don Lang and His Frantic Five, Wee Willie Harris and Lord Rockingham's XI clearly understood the rules of the game: if you were going to perform rock'n'roll, it wasn't enough to sound silly, you had to look silly and act silly as well. It was all terrific fun but, as the programme earnestly sought to imply for the benefit of any adults watching, *harmless*. What was jiving, after all, but a descendant of the gavotte by way of the Gay Gordons?

Commercial radio and television were less inhibited about giving the kids what they wanted. Every night, Radio Luxembourg faded in and out of the nation's teenage bedrooms with its sponsored plugs for discs which were always cut short at the instrumental break (to hear the whole song you had to buy the record), interrupted by ads for Valderma spot cream and the Infa-Draw Method for winning the pools.

ITV's first pop show, Jack Good's 'Oh Boy!', embodied the realisation that

rock'n'roll was a matter of *image* (a word that was to enjoy a considerable vogue as the sixties got under way). It was Good who took away Gene Vincent's check jacket, dressed him in black leather and a medallion and created a sexy young Richard III. He understood as no-one before that the music was nothing without sweat, grease, sneers, leers, throbs and twitches. Indeed it is recorded, perhaps apocryphally, that he stood watching Gene Vincent in the spotlight and muttered 'Limp, you bugger, limp!' Good was ahead of his time, and 'Oh Boy!' didn't last long. Television preferred to sanitise pop with programmes like 'Juke Box Jury' ('Now let's hear Katie Boyle's opinion...').

The cinema had even less fun with the new sound. The Elvis films merge in retrospect into a syrup of cute kids and choreography, in which the great man wears flowers round his neck and plinks a ukelele. It had all started so promisingly: in 1953 Brando as *The Wild One*, asked what he was rebelling about, had snarled 'Whaddya got?' By 1961 *The Young Ones* were all in favour of 'doing the show right here'.

For rock'n'roll, 1961 was a bad year. Not only was Buddy Holly dead, but he had left behind a poisoned chalice, a rock'n'roll record with pizzicato violins on it. The music industrialists were back in control: violins they understood, violins they could handle. They had worked out the formula for turning a pretty boy with a quiff (or possibly a quiff with a pretty boy) into a Top Ten teen heart-throb, and it worked every time. Before long rock'n'roll had been diluted to the point where many spoke of a return to 'nice tunes'.

Nothing seemed impossible for the industry machine. A hyperthyroid ex-chicken-plucker from Philadelphia called Ernest Evans, given a two-year-old song by Hank Ballard and the Mid-nighters, and the new name of Chubby Checker, launched a dance craze that would sweep the western world.

Rock'n'roll dancing was a sort of art form, and you were either good at it or you weren't. When the twist came in, that changed. Everybody could do it, it was new for everybody and we all learned how to do it. It didn't matter if you weren't keen on your partner, you got up and did it. That's really what today's dancing is all about, just a variation on the twist.

▲
Originally promoted as Capital Records' answer to Elvis, Gene Vincent inspired later generations of rockers with his leather-clad hoodlum image.

razzle dazzle

Practising with a bath towel, wiggling backwards and forwards so you got the right movement as if you were rubbing your back with a big bath towel . . .

In fact, the twist was no more a part of teenage culture than the hokey-cokey. It was something your auntie did at parties when she'd had a couple of sherries, something Jacqueline Kennedy was photographed doing with diplomats, and something five-year-olds amused everybody by trying to do and falling over. It was another step towards the taming of the teens.

Styles of clothing, too, were being integrated into the wider market. T. R. Fyvel describes how the 'Teddy uniform' gave way before 'the blue jeans, the windcheaters, the bright raincoats, the gentler, more civilised, immensely vari-egated Italian and continental styles which seemed to confirm and usher in the opening society'.

In 1961, a group of Oxford gradu-ates investigated British teenagers for the *Daily Herald* and summed them up thus:

1 Lacking a rebel spirit
2 Too much like their parents
3 Politically ignorant
4 Bored – so very BORED

The *Daily Telegraph* added its own sur-vey results:

To adults, the people whom their teenage progeny respect will prob-ably be surprising. Sir Winston Churchill easily tops the list. Presi-dent Kennedy comes next . . . Where groups are concerned, parents come first in teenage respect; sportsmen are next, with statesmen and film stars far behind. Teachers come nowhere at all.

There was still hope.

▶ A marathon twist contest in a Harlow dance-hall, February 1962. Perhaps the winner was the last dancer to get bored.

let's think about living

'There was a different kind of poetry and there was often wild free jazz, and there was both the desire and the occasion for people to jump up and shout.'

GO MAN GO!

let's think about living

I was a Teddy boy at school. When I got to art college, within about ten seconds, I realised that Teddy boys didn't go to art college. In fact they were people whose hair went in the opposite direction ...

As Abrams had noticed, teenage culture in the fifties was overwhelmingly working-class. It was the fifteen-year-old school-leavers from the secondary moderns who had the money to spend on smart clothes and pop records. The children of the middle classes, plodding on through grammar school towards a place at college, felt rather left out.

This generation of the brightest and best was prey to a mood which was partly the urge to cry sour grapes at the affluent society, and partly a genuine impatience with the stuffy materialism of Macmillan's Britain. Their relative poverty in the midst of plenty alienated them not only from their working-class contemporaries but also from their doing-very-nicely-thank-you parents, who were buying cars, fridges and washing-machines and urging their children to knuckle down and 'get their qualifications' so that in due course they too could have fitted carpets.

▼ Beatnik style: the French bohemian, English intellectual and US hobo look in a single scene.

The generation gap was further widened by the educational process itself: these sixth-formers were learning about things of which their mums and dads were ignorant. They were liable to come home and babble at the tea-table about T. S. Eliot, Salvador Dali, Jean-Paul Sartre or Leon Trotsky. They poked fun at Dixon of Dock Green and sneered at the new cocktail cabinet. They asked awkward questions about the sagacity of the *Daily Express*, the importance of wearing a collar and tie and the existence of God.

The sensitive seventeen-year-old, feeling the alienation which is a normal part of teenage experience, but feeling it more acutely because of this economic and cultural isolation, was ready for a new philosophy. As it happened, there was one to hand.

It had been thrown together during the early fifties by a loosely-knit group of American writers collectively known as the 'Beat Generation', but the appeal of poets Allen Ginsberg, Gregory Corso and Lawrence Ferlinghetti, and of novelists Jack Kerouac and William Burroughs, had more to do with life-style than with literature. It had to do with aimless travel, nonconformism and the search for the 'ultimate high', which it was hoped might be obtained through Zen Buddhism, saxophones, sex, drink, dope, bongo-drums, growing a beard or any combination thereof.

The young British intellectual and the American beatnik were facing much the same problem. Both were in revolt against a national mood of smug consumerism; both were fascinated by a hedonistic and unselfconscious life-style they could never share: in the British case, that of the working-class teenager; in the American case, that of the 'hip' negro.

Norman Mailer, in a footnote to his classic analysis, *The White Negro*, draws a distinction between the hipster and the beatnik, but by the time the influences had crossed the Atlantic they were thoroughly muddled. Only the purists worried about clicking their fingers on the off-beat, when and when not to wear 'shades' and which drugs you should pretend to be addicted to. The basic drive was really all that mattered, the perennial hunger of the intellectual, 'sicklied o'er with the pale cast of thought', to achieve self-forgetfulness in some mind-blasting cosmic orgasm.

Moreover the stew was further enriched by the addition of Parisian flavourings. Paris, after all, had been the traditional home of bohemianism and now it had acquired an intellectually-respectable philosophy called existentialism. Everybody knew somebody who claimed to understand it, but all that most of its adherents needed to know about it was that it approved of casual sex, Gauloises and Juliette Greco.

I can remember Juliette Greco particularly. I rather fancied looking like Juliette Greco. I had a white fluffy duffle-coat which I used to wear until it practically ran away. I mean you wore the same thing day after day after day. The other thing was black polo-neck sweaters.

'Look Back In Anger' was a big hit at the Royal Court and Jimmy Porter in Osborne's play plays the trumpet a bit and says lines like 'Anyone who hates jazz hates life!' He shouts this at some neighbour who moans about the loudness of his trumpet-playing which actually, whether by accident or design, was not much good. You heard this guy rehearsing and you sympathised somewhat with the complainant, but at that age, lines like that represented the youth rebellion.

These Byronic figures. swapping philosophical bons mots in their seedy salons, were also aware (though they might not have admitted it) that their image impressed the hell out of some rather attractive girls.

I seemed to go in for 'unsuitable' men. I had a taste for shady characters. They were called 'Bohemians'; they spent their time in the cafes in Soho, sitting round talking, drinking red wine and cups of coffee, and most of them were either painters, musicians or 'writing'. Almost everybody was in the middle of or just about to write a book. They were poseurs actually, but nevertheless they were exciting people to meet and talk to, and they educated me. And the hunger for knowledge that there was around at that time!

As well as all this drinking and socialising, there was suddenly the 'sleeping around' bit, and this was the

▲ **Juliette Greco had the cool, worldly, chic image to which beatnik girls aspired.**

◀ **Colin Wilson wrote** *The Outsider* **while living in a sleeping bag on Hampstead Heath.**

rebellion against your parents, you see. You were against your safe middle-class homes. You were doing all these naughty things . . .

I remember hours of sitting and talking in coffee bars about all the things we saw wrong, and particularly about these – as we saw it – empty people living their lives in their suburban houses, looking after their gardens, going to work every day, coming home every night and doing nothing else. And our conversations in the coffee bars were about putting the world to rights.

It was to do with having a beard, wearing thonged sandals and writing poetry. I knew the Prince of the Beatniks. He wrote a book of poems called 'Rave'. It's funny stuff. He sat in this coffee bar in which he had some sort of share, or he was friendly with the owner, and he declaimed poetry. He would start a poem and we would say the next line and he would scribble it down and say 'That's a wonderful line. I'm going to use that.'

Harmonica man ▶ Sonny Boy Williamson, one of the elderly blues greats brought to UK audiences by Chris Barber.

The American beatniks were devotees of modern jazz, and some of their British imitators acquired the addiction to Charlie Parker, Thelonius Monk and John Coltrane.

In certain kinds of modern jazz, especially in be-bop, it was traditional, when a player was really 'going', for the audience to start stamping and shouting 'Go, go, go, man, yeah, wow!', to join in and shout and yawp and screech, and often that sort of orgiastic atmosphere was developed.

Older fans of modern jazz despised all that:

If you were deeply moved you might allow your left earlobe to twitch, but it would be a subtle twitch.

There was a small but growing and very dedicated following in Britain for trad-itional 'New Orleans' jazz, which shared be-bop's virtues of being thor-oughly uncommercial and of furnishing material for endless discussions about the finer points of obscure recordings. It had additional advantages: it had tunes you could remember, it had rhythms you

could dance to and there were British bands which could play it passably well.

Like skiffle, the trad boom in Britain began with Ken Colyer who, as George Melly said in his book *Owning Up*: 'established the totems and taboos of traditional jazz, the piano-less rhythm section, the relentless four to the bar banjo, the loud but soggy thump of the bass drum'. Other bands followed, notably those of Chris Barber, Alex Welsh and Cy Laurie. The latter per-formed in a large basement club in Soho, which attracted a regular crowd of beat-niks, art students and layabouts. Clubs like Cy Laurie's, Sam Widges, the Nucleus, the Gyre and Gimble or the Farm established the principle of the 'all-nighter' and gave the new youth culture its seedbed. Some went there for the music, some to sleep, some to smoke a little marijuana (although 'reefers' were still the stuff of myth and legend rather than the everyday indulgence they were to become later in the sixties). At the same time, similar clubs were opening in the provinces: the celebrated Cavern in Liverpool, for example, started in January 1957 as a jazz club.

Trad was a short-lived obsession, killed by its own popularity. By the time Acker Bilk and Kenny Ball had started

scoring hits with their prettified toot-lings and jaunty stompings, the music had lost its authenticity and therefore its appeal. While it lasted, however, it made two important bequests to the youth culture that was to follow: one, already mentioned, was the cellar club; the other was the all-day festival held in the open air or under canvas. There is also a respectable case to be made for the thesis that without trad there would have been no British rhythm'n'blues boom, and therefore no Rolling Stones, no Eric Clapton and no Who.

Because the beatnik philosophy valued music less for its intrinsic qual-ities than for its 'authenticity', it smiled upon every style of jazz, blues or folk which could plausibly claim to be 'the real thing'. It was Chris Barber who introduced Big Bill Broonzy to British concert-goers in 1955 and who later compèred a series of 'Folk Blues Fes-tivals' which assembled some of the most stunning line-ups of talent ever to share a stage and which created an enthusiastic following for the blues. Artists like Sonny Boy Williamson and Lightnin' Hopkins were similarly pleased to be introduced to an adulation and an income they could never expect at home, and they came back regularly to

play the cellar clubs in the early sixties. It is significant, however, that Muddy Waters, a virtuoso of the amplified Southside Chicago style, was obliged to play acoustic guitar on his first British tour because the audiences clung to a romantic vision of the sharecropper on his cabin porch, twanging lonesome melodies into the delta dusk, and did not care to be reminded that the blues had grown up, moved north and turned sassy. A cartoon of the time shows a blind, black, geriatric guitarist with a wooden leg, wearing prison stripes and a ball and chain, and one beatnik saying to another, 'He's good ... but is he authentic?'

That was one way to achieve acceptance; another was to be pol-itically sound. Pete Seeger, who had more in common musically with Burl Ives than with Leadbelly, was embraced because he'd paid his dues on the road with Woodie Guthrie and had been banned from American television for his left-of-centre affiliations. Ewan McColl (real name Jimmy Miller) was the Eng-lish equivalent, a writer of plangent pas-tiches in the folk-protest idiom which glorified fishermen, navvies, gypsies and other simple-but-profound characters.

Songs of the Civil Rights movement

◀The Chris Barber Band with singer George Melly and Lonnie Donegan on banjo.

(such as 'We Shall Overcome'), Appalachian ballads, African lullabies ('Kumbaya My Lord, Kumbaya') and songs about the advisability of unilateral nuclear disarmament were all grist to the three-chord mill. The same folkies who would argue themselves hoarse about the 'correct' version of 'Barbara Allen' would happily sing 'H-Bomb Thunder', often in a countrified accent meant to sound more 'authentic'.

In 1956, the year of Suez, John Osborne's Jimmy Porter had complained that there were 'no good, brave causes left', but it was not long after that political watershed that a group of radical intellectuals, Osborne among them, launched the biggest 'good, brave cause' of the lot, the Campaign for Nuclear Disarmament.

I can remember vividly the day I learned about it from this boy at school, and him coming out with this bit about an atom bomb and how many people would be killed, and for some amazing reason it was completely news to me. We became absolutely terrified at the reality of how small we were in the universe and how powerless, and the enormity of this bomb and the terror of it.

We were tremendously idealistic and just thought that if we marched we could really be part of this big movement that was actually going to achieve something.

The number who marched the sixty miles between Aldermaston and London in CND's Easter pilgrimage increased from 10,000 in 1958 to an estimated 100,000 by 1961. The new recruits changed the character of the movement; they made it younger, less earnest, more subversive and more fun. A *Guardian* correspondent on the 1962 march reported that 95% of the marchers were under twenty-one, and a high proportion of them under eighteen. Teenagers were joining the direct-action splinter group, the Committee of 100, and learning the delights of sitting down, going limp and being bundled into police vans. In 1963 a group called 'Spies for Peace' revealed the locations of a number of theoretically secret bunkers, the 'Regional Seats of Government', one of which – in the appropriately named village of Wargrave – happened to be on the line of the Aldermaston march and was gleefully picketed. It was becoming easier for cynics to say that the march was more of a carnival of irresponsible youth than a political statement.

Young protesters ▶ cool their toes in Trafalgar Square at the climax of the 1960 Aldermaston March.

I can remember arriving at Hyde Park, a massive convergence of people on Hyde Park, and the people were played in by jazz bands. And then I can remember lots of dancing and people sitting around and resting after this really quite strenuous march. I think probably I was more interested in that than in the speeches . . .

At the end of his radio documentary about the 1961 march, René Cutforth gave his devastating reply to the accusation that the demonstrators were nothing more than a crowd of ignorant teenagers. It is worth quoting in full:

Consider for a moment the times we middle-aged men have lived through in this monstrous century: first, the huge, terrible casualty lists of the First World War; then the mass unemployment, the misery and the injustice of the early thirties; then the spectacle of Europe under the heel of a murdering maniac, Belsen, Auschwitz, the Jews in the gas chambers; then another war, then Hiroshima, Nagasaki, and finally, for us, an exhausted, meaningless state, intent on the 'lolly'.

In medical matters there is a principle called tolerance: if some poisons are fed to a human being over a long period, he acquires a tolerance of them and can survive a lethal dose, though his whole metabolism may have to change to meet the challenge. The young are those who have so far never breathed the poisons we've had to contrive to survive, and their minds are unclouded by them. With every increase of tolerance, we have lost the human sensitivity, and now it seems to me quite possible that these marchers, whatever their impact on the bomb or the possible future impact of the bomb upon them, these Aldermaston marchers may well already be the only people still left alive in Britain.

The 'bearded boys' with 'banjos on their backs' did not spend all their time organising fund-raising jumble sales in Quaker meeting rooms and leafletting shopping centres; they were part of a movement that was broader than any political campaign, and broader too than the rather older beatnik groups which had established its stance and style. They were called 'ravers' and they had a loose uniform: skin-tight jeans, a sloppy sweater, long hair, perhaps a bowler hat decorated with a CND symbol, and a hand-rolled cigarette. The beard was a clue to which sex, in any particular instance, was wearing the outfit.

I always insisted on wearing my dad's jumper and he was huge, so I mean the jumper used to come down to my knees, and if you had a bit of string tied round your middle, the old ladies would think you were absolutely diabolical.

I got caned for wearing a duffle-coat. I insisted on buying a duffle-coat and wearing it to school, and it was an offence to wear a duffle-coat, a caneable offence.

Everyone said 'Ooh it would be great if we went down to Brighton' and so we used to hitch-hike and you just used to sit on the beach and eventually people would turn up in ones and twos, and sometimes they would have a guitar or a clarinet or a trumpet or whatever and we used to dance on the beach and get all these old girls saying 'Ooh, they're those ones that don't wash, they were in the paper!'

To 'rave' was to dance to trad jazz in an eccentric fashion that defies description; it somehow combined elements of jiving, cake-walking, skipping and the minuet in a movement both stately and graceless; but to be a 'raver' was a matter of life-style, either full- or part-time:

We only used to be weekend ravers. We used to just go down for the weekend and spend the night under Brighton pier. I mean, we were picked up for vagrancy once on Brighton front, Brenda and I. I was supposed to be staying at Brenda's for the night in Balham and there I was being picked up on Brighton beach for vagrancy!

The full-time ravers were the first 'drop-outs', travelling the country with dirty sleeping-bags and weatherbeaten thumbs, supporting themselves by

*let's think
about living*

casual labouring jobs and the charity of friends. As the sixties got under way, these latter-day tramps mutated into something else, a tougher lot altogether than the grammar school and art college brigade; older, scruffier and longer-haired, either they had done a better job of shedding their bourgeois backgrounds or they had never had them to begin with. Some were notable for wearing earrings, tattoos or needle-marks, others for walking about on bare and unwashed feet. They had names like Gipsy Dave, Frenchie or Mad Mick, but they were collectively known as 'dossers' and the weekend ravers viewed them with considerable awe.

Dossers seemed to know things: they spoke of sexual liaisons both complex and casual, of weird drugs and obscure blues singers and they always seemed to know where the party was going to be next weekend. In summer they migrated to the coast, being particularly fond of Cornwall. Having trekked like lemmings to the western-most tip of Britain, the dossers spent the summer sitting on the harbour wall at St Ives, scowling at the holiday-makers and blowing mouth-organs.

Many of them were still there in 1967 when their time came round again and suddenly they were hippies. Some of them are there yet.

how do you do it?

'So the Cavern got fuller and fuller, sweatier and sweatier and louder and louder, because eventually the duffle-coats left and they just took the place over.'

THE BEATLES

how do you do it?

And then the first thing that happens is this: we're doing this gig and John gets off the bus and he's got this huge box with like a red light on the top and it's a fifteen-watt amplifier, and we'd always known his guitar was electric but it just had this silver thing on it, you know, and a couple of little knobs that didn't do anything. He plugs it in and starts to play ELECTRIC GUITAR. Astonishing! 'Cos it's loud, you know? 'Cos before, you know, it was chanka chanka chanka and if the clientele got a bit ratty about it they could drown you out . . . 'Rubbish! Get off!' But now you discover the secret of Status Quo and Rainbow . . . 'I'll be louder than they buggers!' BYOIOIOING!

The beat group evolved, largely unnoticed by the entertainment industry at large, in the five years between the death of skiffle and the explosion of Merseybeat. It was a product of technological change and musical frustration; do-it-yourself rock'n'roll for a generation that was denied access to the real thing.

It did not start in Liverpool; Merseybeat was a second-stage refinement of a formula which was already established. The first successful beat groups, outfits like Johnny Kidd and the Pirates, Mike Berry and the Outlaws or Jimmy Powell and the Dimensions, were already veterans of the dance-hall and package-tour circuits by the time the Beatles made their first record.

So why was Liverpool important? The answer has more to do with quantity than with quality. What was happening in Liverpool, and to a lesser extent in other cities (especially ports), was a sudden vast increase in the number of young lads getting together to make music; that, in turn, came about because of the new availability of the instruments, amplification and the hire-purchase required.

What you ended up with was three guitars going into the same amp; the drummer is added and he's got a proper kit 'cos his dad's a headmaster, so you've got rhythm guitar, lead guitar, bass guitar and drums. Then comes the rise of the P.A., 'cos for a long time you're stuck with whatever microphone and speaker the hall – the church hall or the pub or whatever it is –

has. That's a great leap forward because the group now becomes self-contained. And now you buy a Transit 'cos it's too big for a car. The Ford Transit is the vehicle. You put the gear in the Transit, go off to the gig, put up the P.A., put up your mikes, plug in your amp, and you played . . .

There was a group every square yard in this city. The local scene was so vibrant, and just about every local area had two or three halls which could provide venues; I mean, venues was the name of the game. These people could live on a fiver a week, you know, as long as they could get a couple of turn-outs.

You know, everybody knew somebody who was playing in a group, so there was a kind of democratised stardom. People wanted to give you the chance as well: when you look at the histories of some of those local rock'n'roll groups, the aunties who came forward with the initial twenty quid! They wanted to give the kids a ride because everyone had just been through such a hard time, and that makes for people saying 'Oh, give him a guitar! We've just fought Hitler, for Chrissake! That's what we did it for . . .'

By the summer of 1961, the group scene in Liverpool was already lively enough to support a weekly newspaper, *Merseybeat*, and the established cellar clubs in the city were starting to book groups as well as jazz bands.

There were a lot of old jazz clubs in this town, like the Cavern and the Iron Door, where the long-hairs with long scarves and duffle coats and CND badges used to dance a strange dance to these boozed-up versions of New Orleans jazz bands. They weren't all that much good but people had a good time and those were the clubs that were taken over by the rising beat generation. But I think there was a fair frisson when the old clientele saw the Merseyssippi Seven moved over by Gerry and the Pacemakers and the Beatles and the Big Three.

The sound was such that it took you about twelve hours to recuperate. You know, when you came outside, you were talking to your mates and all you could see was mouths

moving up and down, because you weren't going at twenty watts so you couldn't hear anything.

Just as technology had made possible the four-man self-contained rock'n'roll group, it now gradually began to change the style of the music. The development of the bass speaker cabinet in particular made the stomach-thumping beat of the bass guitar the dominant sound, above which all the other ingredients had to struggle to be heard. The group therefore needed a high-pitched, clanging lead guitar, a leather-throated lead vocal and two or three voices shouting out the choruses. Partly for this reason, and partly through the influence of black American vocal groups, two- or three-part harmony singing became a feature of the Mersey sound.

Virtually every song that every Liverpool group performed in the pre-Beatles gestation period was copied from an American record; hardly any of them had been British hits. From the point of view of the audiences, unfamiliar with the originals, it was as though the Liverpool groups had exclusive access to the best rock'n'roll songs ever written, and performed them the way they were meant to be performed.

The sailors arriving back in this town used to bring, along with the Fender guitars that you couldn't get anywhere else, a lot of songs on record that people didn't hear because they weren't in the pop charts here.

You were thrashing along in a pub and some bloke comes up and says 'Have you ever heard Chuck Berry?' You say 'Oh yeah, I heard him on Radio Luxembourg one time.' He says 'Here you are, here's an album. Fifteen bob.' You say 'Yeah, I'll have that!' And you go home and that one album is precious. You learned every note until you could play it exactly . . .

There was a basic repertoire of fifteen or twenty songs that more or less every band would be doing, you know, things like the Coasters' 'Poison Ivy' and perhaps a bit of Chuck Berry, and you'd go and see the bands and they'd all be doing the same sort of stuff. You didn't really go expecting to be surprised.

These keen but limited rock'n'roll revivalists might have remained in this musical blind alley, had it not been for the changes that were taking place in American pop music during the early sixties. For years the British pop industry had kept itself going by providing teen idols who turned out cover versions of songs that were simultaneously being churned out by American teen idols; but now the US teen dream scene was on its last legs and a new kind of music was coming through, of which the Craig Douglasses and the Mark Wynters were unaware and which they couldn't have attempted anyway. The new sounds were coming from independent record companies like Berry Gordy's Detroit-based Tamla label. The Beatles *were* aware of this music and could make a passable attempt at reproducing it in their all-purpose bass-thump-and-tenor-harmonies style. In fact, thanks to their gruelling apprenticeship on the Hamburg club circuit, they could tackle almost anything from Carl Perkins rockabilly to 'A Taste of Honey', including material pinched from the Shirelles, Marvelettes, Donays, Miracles, Barrett Strong, Chuck Willis, Larry Williams, Isley Brothers, Arthur Alexander and many more; all great songs, all ranging from moderately to totally obscure.

It was this eclectic competence which gave the Beatles their head start. In itself it was not enough to sustain

how do you do it?

▼ **Pop merchandisers were beginning to spot possibilities. One gimmick: a sew-on badge for the anorak sleeve.**

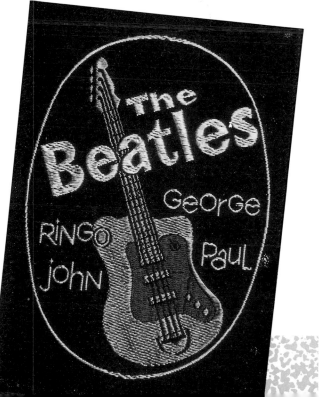

them as stars, and once they had broken through they switched gradually to songs they had written themselves. Their contemporaries who couldn't or wouldn't make this transition inevitably faded away, having opened the British market to the very sounds they were borrowing.

There was one more ingredient that was crucial, and it had to do with the relationship between the groups and their followers. Whereas previous musical idols had been remote, glamorous figures to their fans, the Mersey groups had evolved out of teenage gangs and still, in a sense, belonged to them.

When you saw the Beatles on stage there was a continuous kind of across-the-barriers banter going on. We used to throw toilet rolls at them and they used to throw them back.

Because they had arrived through sessions in pubs and clubs, it seemed natural for groups to wear their everyday dress on stage, to perform with a smouldering cigarette or glass of beer on top of the amplifier and to argue with the audience about which song they should do next. Their stage personalities were genuine, and this fact was as important to their later success as the music itself.

There really wasn't a great deal of attempt to put on a show. It was just fairly sweaty and direct and they just got up and played and stomped about a bit and the crowd did the same...

Mayall formed his ► Blues Breakers in 1962. Although Clapton jammed with them in those early days, he didn't join the band until 1966.

Jammed together on the Cavern's crowded dance-floor, the beat fans developed a new dance, the Cavern Stomp, an eyeball-to-eyeball shuffle in which the participants linked fingers and swayed their forearms like metronomes.

The clubs weren't licensed so there wasn't any booze; the main high was the music. And the guys in the band were just like you were: they probably had daytime jobs, they couldn't afford flash stage-gear — maybe suits or perhaps a prized plastic jerkin and a pink tab-collar shirt.

The Beatles' success (their second release, 'Please Please Me', went to number two in March 1963) focussed the attentions of the pop establishment on Merseyside. The record company representatives arrived clutching cheque books and Liverpool street-maps with Mathew Street marked by a cross. The realisation dawned that all Denmark Street had to do was take the groups, polish them up, render them a little less offensive and peddle the product. Its first instinct was to make the phenomenon fit the preconceived pattern, so it went for acts in two categories: the cheeky and the crooners. Gerry (of Gerry and the Pacemakers), Freddie (of Freddie and the Dreamers) and Herman (of Herman's Hermits) — the latter two both from Manchester — had all the cheeky charm that Tommy Steele had brought to bear in the first wave of rock'n'roll. Balladeers like Cilla Black and Billy J. Kramer fitted the alternative stereotype, with the additional qualification that they could claim acquaintance with the Fab Four.

For all these attempts to assimilate the beat groups to the Tin Pan Alley formula, some things did change for good as a result of the Merseybeat boom. The group became the standard unit of pop currency; a record's 'backing' became extremely important (so much that 'I liked/didn't like the backing' became a 'Juke Box Jury' cliché). It became the exception rather than the rule for a group not to write its own material. New club and dance-hall circuits had been opened up which would supply a steady if exhausting living to anyone with a van-load of amplifiers and a modicum of talent. In short, the pop industry had been obliged to adjust

to giving the fans what they wanted, rather than what it thought it could flog to them . . . up to a point.

When long-haired blues fanatics met beat group technology, the result was the early sixties rhythm'n'blues boom. It started in a small way as an offshoot of trad: Chris Barber experimented with Chicago-style blues combos, as did the influential guitarist Alexis Korner and a balding, middle-aged panel-beater called Cyril Davies, who played convincing blues harmonica. The impulse to reproduce the music, however, was merely an extension of the passion for collecting the records, a sort of aural equivalent of train-spotting. Then younger musicians began to gather round this nucleus and eventually the regular R'n'B sessions at the Marquee and other London venues would feature such dedicated unknowns as Nicky Hopkins, Graham Bond, John Mayall, Charlie Watts, Mick Jagger, Keith Richard and Brian Jones. Everybody knew everybody else and they all loved the blues.

London was the centre and set the style for what outsiders dismissed as 'the Bo Diddley bands': the Kinks, Yardbirds, Pretty Things and Rolling Stones, although Newcastle's Animals and Belfast's Them (whose lead singer was Van Morrison) were evidence that the blues boom was not merely metropolitan.

Because groups were big business in 1963–4, the R'n'B bands rode out of the esoteric world of the club all-nighter and into the pop charts on the same tidal wave. When the wave receded, it was those who had smoothed the jagged edges of their style and begun to write their own songs who survived as big-time pop stars. The hard-liners retained their poverty along with their purity and kept the torch alight for the next wave of blues revivalism towards the end of the decade.

Despite the fact that they went through the same 'sign 'em up, clean 'em up, book 'em out' mill as the Mersey groups, the blues bands retained elements of a rather different image. With a leavening of art students and a general flavour of beatnikism about them, they had a more self-consciously rebellious stance than the cheeky chappies of the northern beat groups. The difference persisted: in June 1965 the Beatles were awarded the MBE; in July 1965 the Stones were fined for pissing against a wall.

The songs were different too: the Merseybeat vocalist was concerned to plead with his 'baby' to 'come on home' and 'be his girl' (wo-wo-yeah-yeah); the R'n'B singer, meanwhile, told his 'woman' not to 'dog him around' or else (with much muttering about 'de ole graveyard', the 'gipsy woman' who 'done tole me' this, that or the other, and an assortment of black cat bones, back-door men and midnight ramblers). It was all very macho and the aggressive pose was maintained even after the lyrics changed to 'Hey, you, get off my cloud!'

When I first saw Mick Jagger I remember being absolutely knocked out by his strutting about and his arrogance. He was the sort of person I'd like to have been but I never thought I could actually be that good.

The Stones were different. When you saw Jagger performing, to have somebody who had the audacity to stand up there and move the way he did! I remember being glued to 'Top of the Pops' the first time I saw Mick Jagger. I was absolutely mesmerised by his body and I remember my grandma saying 'Good God, look at him! Look at him! His trousers'll fall down soon and then we shall see

▼ The Stones looked meaner, leaner and a good deal shaggier than the Beatles. One was not allowed to like both groups.

how do
you do it?

good, white rhythm'n'blues band, whereas the Beatles wanted to be something completely new. They knew where their roots were but they knew they were going to the toppermost of the poppermost, and they pulled it off!

The national Press did not discover Beatlemania until October 1963, when the group's second number-one record propelled them onto the television variety show 'Sunday Night at the London Palladium'. (Incidentally, it was typical of the Rolling Stones that when they appeared on the same programme they embarrassed everybody at the end by refusing to climb aboard the revolving stage and wave.) The *Daily Telegraph* noted:

Crowds of chanting, screaming teenagers last night besieged the London Palladium where the Beatles, the Liverpool 'pop' musical group, were appearing in the ITV show.

Some girls forced their way into the theatre through a back entrance, but left when threatened with a fire hose. Other teenagers climbed onto the theatre roof before police eventually cleared the crowds.

Having mulled over this and other similar incidents for a couple of weeks, the *Telegraph* delivered itself of an editorial opinion:

Is there not something a bit frightening in whole masses of young people, all apparently so suggestible, so volatile and rudderless? What material here for the maniac's shaping: Hitler would have disapproved, but he could have seen what in other circumstances might be made of it ... Most cultural fads and fashions are fairly absurd. More absurd than most are fashions which, like those of today, are largely set from 'below'. Professors, writers, intellectuals, bishops, all take care to be discreetly 'with it', fully conversant and in sympathy with all that wells and throbs up from the slums beneath them. The cultural tone of society is normally set by the leisured and moneyed classes.

▲
Vaguely mod, very loyal, Stones fans wait for a glimpse of their idols in the summer of 1965.

'We screamed because it was the done thing. We egged each other on.'

something!' ...'But Gran, he's fantastic!' And of course the more disgusted she was, the more attractive I found him. Yes, I think Jagger was something else. Everything about him spelled sex.

You know, when you look at the early Stones, what they're trying to be is a very

Our teenagers have leisure and money. What sort of cultural tone are they setting?

This rhetorical question was answered in two ways. The music critic of *The Times* compared Lennon and McCartney with Schubert and Mahler (' ...''That Boy'' ... with its chains of pandiatonic clusters ... and the flat submediant key-switches ... the Aeolian cadence at the end of ''Not a Second Time'' ... ') while *The Sunday Times* said they were the greatest composers since Beethoven. The Beatles' fans answered it more straightforwardly with a long, loud, many-throated scream.

I think it was something to do with letting off a terrific amount of energy. I had so much energy then, we all did, so what better idea than to go and see a group and scream it all out that way? It was almost therapeutic really.

I remember screaming at the television screen, along with my friends. We'd be into a chorus of screams until someone stuck their head round the door and said 'Shut up, for goodness' sake'.

Oh you were absolutely in there and you were part of it. If I hadn't been part of it I would think it was totally ludicrous when you see it on film, but it was just what everybody else was doing and it was, I suppose, sex actually, that it was about. I think it was. I'm pretty sure.

The Dionysian mood extended to the dance-floor, where the 'shake', which had taken over from the twist, the stomp and the hully-gully, resembled the trance-inducing twitchings of a voodoo seance.

You had to shake your head very vigorously from side to side. There was no way you could get away without a thumping headache at the end of the evening.

In February 1964 the Beatles arrived in the US and neatly reversed the pattern of 1956. Their impact on a nation which had spent three months in mourning for its president was as sudden and profound as had been that of Bill Haley and Elvis Presley on Britain; rock'n'roll was coming home, having grown and changed to the point where America thought it was greeting a stranger.

Meanwhile, back in the UK, the groups were consolidating their hold on the domestic market. The Top Ten for 14 March 1964 was the first ever all-British hit parade. As Beatlemania grew to unprecedented proportions, Paul Johnson, in a choleric but prescient article in the *New Statesman*, identified what was happening to the 'establishment':

So long as the Beatles were just another successful showbiz team, the pillars of society could afford to ignore them, beyond bestowing the indulgent accolade of a slot in the Royal Variety Performance. But then came the shock announcement

how do you do it?

March 1965, and the Beatles, plus wives, leave Heathrow for their Scandinavian tour. The fans, said a radio commentator, were 'like starlings'.

that they were earning £6,250,000 a year – and, almost simultaneously, they got the stamp of approval from America.

This was quite a different matter. At once they became not only part of the export trade but an electorally valuable property. Sir Alec Home promptly claimed credit for them, and was as promptly accused by Mr Wilson of political clothes-stealing. Conservative candidates have been officially advised to mention them whenever possible in their speeches. The Queen expressed concern about the length of Ringo's hair. Young diplomats at our Washington embassy fought for their autographs. A reporter described them as 'superb ambassadors for Britain'.

The growing public approval of anti-culture is itself, I think, a reflection of the new cult of youth. Bewildered by a rapidly changing society, excessively fearful of becoming out of date, our leaders are increasingly turning to young people as guides and mentors – or, to vary the metaphor, as geiger-counters to guard them against the perils of mental obsolescence ... Whatever youth likes must be good: the supreme crime, in politics and culture alike, is not to be 'with it'.

Fortunately for the teenagers, who felt as strongly as any generation the need to be in revolt against their fuddy-duddy elders, there were still plenty of 'pillars of society' who turned up their noses at the Beatles. Lord Willis in the House of Lords pleaded with the Government to launch a new 'cultural campaign', declaring that 'we cannot leave this field to pop merchants and the bingo boys'. He spoke of a firm which had turned from making plastic busts of Shakespeare to making plastic busts of the Beatles. 'There is no sign of an end to the deluge', he cried, 'This is not culture, it is a cult. This is a cheap, plastic, candyfloss substitute for culture, and somebody should have the courage to say so.'

If anything, this was slightly preferable to the process Johnson described, the pathetic attempt by oldsters (who thought a Fender was something you put around a fireplace) to climb aboard the Beatles' bandwagon. The attempt was bound to fail, precisely because John, Paul, George and Ringo were essentially of and for the nation's teenagers. Their constituency was the young and the attitude of the grown-ups, be it approval, disapproval or an eagerness to make money out of the whole thing, was largely irrelevant to the festival of youth that was taking place.

Because of course the Beatles weren't just music, this is the whole point; they were symbols of teenagers. I mean they were us up there. And Paul McCartney particularly in my case, you identified very strongly with him and you'd think 'What does he feel about this issue?' and you'd read it and you'd think 'Oh yes, that's what I think', and you would try and remember how he behaved, that sort of schoolboyish charm and that sort of manner and a smile, and you'd be using all that when you were talking to girls. I mean they really were a sort of Emily Post etiquette for us, you know. We learned how to behave from them.

'A Hard Day's Night', I think, is one of the most important films of the sixties. There's a classic scene where there's the old guy with the newspaper, and that was one side, and there's the Beatles on the other side, and they're sitting a few feet away in a train but actually they're miles and miles apart.

The scene ends with the following exchange:

Man: I fought the war for your sort.
Ringo: I bet you're sorry you won.

he's so fine

'I remember once I got all dressed up to go out and I had one clean shirt. I was cleaning my shoes and I noticed some spots of boot polish on the shirt. I didn't go out. That's how seriously we all took it.'

he's so fine

The last week of March 1964 was an eventful one in teenage history.

On Saturday, the first pirate radio station began transmitting non-stop pop from a ship called the *Caroline* moored outside territorial waters, off the coast of Essex.

On Sunday, on that very coast, there occurred in Clacton what the Chief Constable at the time described as 'several acts of wanton and purposeless damage'. The *Daily Express* put it more vividly:

A thousand rioting teenage 'wild ones' brawled, rampaged and fought their way through the streets of a seaside resort yesterday.

▼ **Brighton, Whit Monday, 1964. A Bank Holiday tradition begins to emerge.**

Sixty people were arrested over the Easter weekend, several people got thumped, damage to property was estimated at £500 and this unremarkable affray passed into legend as the first mod-rocker riot.

On Tuesday, the Government published a bill which would prohibit the unauthorised possession of amphetamine pills. A pocketful of previously-legal 'purple hearts' would soon cost you anything up to six months in jail.

In a single week, teenagers had acquired their own broadcasting service and witnessed the first twitches of establishment hysteria over drugs, while those of them who had never heard of mods or rockers (the majority) had been offered by the media a choice of two do-it-yourself teenage rebellion kits.

By May, the teenagers of Britain had made their decisions and sorted themselves out. A schoolteacher reported to *New Society* that over half the boys in his technical school had aligned themselves with one group or the other, while the committed proportions at nearby secondary moderns were even greater.

By August, the words 'mod' and 'rocker' were widely known outside the UK, if not understood, and the Pope was able to tell an audience of Italian Rover Scouts that 'the unhappy faces ... of the 'mods' and 'rockers' ... reveal profound, piteous dramas filled with sorrow, lack of trust, vice, badness and delinquency.'

His Holiness may have been unaware as he spoke that the seeds of the modernist style had blown to Britain from Italy some five years earlier. It all began with the import of cheap Italian suits cut in a bizarre fashion: short, box jackets ('bum-freezers'), narrow lapels and drain-pipe trousers. Worn with winklepicker shoes, white socks, 'slim Jim' knitted ties, silk shirts and blow-waved hair-cuts, these became the last word in sartorial elegance in the post-Ted era. The look was chosen at the time as a mark of distinction not only from the outmoded Edwardian style, but also as a reaction against the scruffiness of the trad jazz brigade. It bespoke a fondness for modern as opposed to traditional jazz, and its adherents therefore called themselves 'modernists'.

From the beginning it was a dandified image. There was a touch of 'What if I am?' about it. An anonymous teenage girl, interviewed for the radio in 1961, observed that although 'the modernist boys are smarter, they're getting as conceited as what the girls are ... always looking in mirrors and patting their hair down and putting it into place.' The secret of the mod hair-style in those pre-hair-spray days was sugar and water.

You'd leave it on all night, then wash it out in the morning before you went to work. That way you got a perfect little parting down the front.

Perfection was the aim all right. The most dedicated of the dandies in the East End of London, soon moved on from ready-to-wear and started designing their own tailored suits.

If you were poor you had to start with Burtons, but then you went up to guys

whose fathers were tailors and you had to bribe them to get your suits made. You'd copy little ideas out of Italian magazines, or something you'd spot in a film. French films were very much in vogue then.

A friend of mine took it so seriously. He turned up one day and he had a stripey jumper, a bike, a beret, and he even had some onions. He was just the epitome. He was an A1 mod, that one.

As Pete Townshend remembers:

This kid used to work in the bank at the top of the road. He had very short hair, always wore a nice suit, a very clean-cut kid. He was also an outrageous mod. He was very alert, because he was pilled out of his head all day. His hair wasn't just short, it was also a very subtle French crew, so it was very sharp and in fashion. His suit was made out of Tonik, which was very important. It had to be Tonik. It would be in that month's colour, which would be either dark brown or dark blue. The lapels would be the exact correct width. It might be a two-button jacket or a single-button jacket. It might be a three-button jacket with the top and bottom buttons left undone – whatever happened to be the vogue at the time. It might have single pockets on either side. They might be straight or slanted. There was a craze, also, for several secret inside pockets to a suit, so one tended to fold one's jacket over and put one's hand in one's pocket, holding the jacket open so that people could see that you had the right number of inside pockets ... And yet he would still get a job in a bank. He had to have a job to spend all this money on dope and clothes. And nobody knew except me and him and a few other people. It was a way that people could be legitimate, fit into society, and yet at the same time be outrageously fashionable and in-crowd.

Modernists may have taken their collective name from modern jazz, but it expressed far more than their musical preferences. At the start of the sixties, 'modern' was a word that stood for a whole complex of ideas and attitudes, all of them optimistic.

In 1959, *Queen Magazine* asked:

Have you woken up yet? Do you know that you are living in a new world? Here we are, twenty years after the war started, in an age better even than any of our grandfathers can remember ... We don't want you to miss it. Don't wait until years after to realise you have lived in a remarkable age – the age of BOOM.

The first and most obvious sign of the boom was the comparative affluence of youth. A bright fifteen-year-old could walk into any of a dozen reasonably well-paid white-collar jobs. Mods

▲
It would be uncool to discuss the subject, but somehow they have to decide which bird will ride on which scooter.

enhanced the effect of this spending-power in two ways. One was by purchasing cheap clothes – a shirt from Littlewoods or a check jacket from Burtons – and altering them in subtle ways to make them special. The other was by shop-lifting. But by whatever legal or illegal means, the aim was to look cool, sophisticated and stylish, to walk into the Bastille coffee bar and be admired by other mods. At the beginning there wasn't much more to it than that. If that had remained the essence of mod, it would surely have passed unremarked. But during those early years the nucleus was being bombarded by other sources of energy; in particular by a certain kind of music – rhythm'n'blues – and by a certain chemical compound – amphetamine.

he's so fine

I remember once going to see Jimmy Reed at the Flamingo and I couldn't believe it – and he couldn't believe it! He came in the Flamingo and he was still in his overcoat, he didn't take his overcoat off, and his manager was next to him, and they were bewildered. They were playing, standing up in the middle of the crowd, and there were all these kids around, the mods, that they couldn't relate to at all. These young, white, European kids looking at Jimmy Reed, idolising him, standing there with their mouths open saying 'It's Jimmy Reed!' And he's standing there, this black guy from wherever he's from, and you could see he was a bit edgy about it. The manager was thinking right, we'll do this, grab the money and run, Jimmy, before they lynch us . . . It was amazing though. He was absolutely idolised, surrounded by these doting fans, this quite old, black, blues singer. That was great.

Mods liked R'n'B because the best records were obscure and hard to get. They liked it because the rhythms were rather more subtle than those of ordinary pop, and therefore more difficult and rewarding to dance to. (It was important that being a mod should never be easy.) They liked it because the tone of most of the songs was cool, hip, knowing, *grown-up*, as opposed to the gee-whizz gaucherie of most pop lyrics. They also liked rhythm'n'blues because its most authentic practitioners, both black and white, tended to be middle-aged and physically unattractive. There was nobody up on stage who might cause their narcissism to tremble, which is another reason why proper mods weren't too keen on the younger groups like the Rolling Stones and the Yardbirds. God forbid a mod bird should be moved to squeal at a singer!

The obscurity was the main thing. Veterans of London's Scene Club still speak in awed tones about the record collection of the resident disc-jockey, Guy Stephens. They were very snobbish about the matter of authenticity. When the Rolling Stones walked into the Twisted Wheel Club in Manchester, shortly after the release of their first LP, disc-jockey Roger Eagle took pleasure in playing, one after another, all the songs from the record *in their original versions*. The Stones scowled but the mods understood.

Mod musical tastes had to keep changing because the pop industry kept catching up. They'd liked modern jazz at first, but after Brubeck had a Top Ten hit with 'Take Five', ordinary kids got into modern jazz, so mods moved on to R'n'B. Supply followed demand and Pye started putting out the Chess catalogue, the authentic Chicago stuff, on their red and yellow 'International' label. The Chess compilation album 'Rhythm and Blues All Stars' was the definitive

▼ **Residents at the Flamingo Club, Georgie Fame and the Blue Flames mixed black and white musicians to produce jazzy R'n'B with huge mod-appeal.**

mod party record for a time. But then it got too easy again and the mods moved on. In a few short years they picked up and dropped again such diverse styles as sweet soul (Jerry Butler, the Impressions), Tamla Motown, blue beat (the Jamaican precursor of ska and reggae), James Brown, Otis Redding and even the more obscure California surfing records (which is how the Who came to be doing 'Bucket T' on 'Ready Steady Go'.) In fact anything would do so long as it had a tricky beat and *nobody else knew about it.*

Teddy boys sometimes got drunk, beatniks occasionally smoked a 'reefer' or three, but mod was the first British youth culture to be shaped and conditioned from the beginning by the effects of a particular drug.

Amphetamines were widely prescribed in the early sixties. You could get them for depression, for anxiety or just to help you diet. In fact, almost anyone qualified for a prescription. Supplies were therefore cheap and plentiful.

I had a friend who was working in a big firm that produced Benzedrine, and he'd go onto the production line and chat up a couple of the girls and come away with a thousand of these pills every week. And he'd take them over to the club and sell them. Most of the time they were very cheap. For a couple of shillings you could buy enough drugs to keep you high for three or four days.

I'd take probably eight of these capsules, which would keep me awake for two nights. And of course the next two days at work, Monday and Tuesday, were pretty horrible. And by the time Wednesday came I was looking forward to the weekend. You get a tremendous amount of energy from it, and you're talking all the time. You think you're a genius. It's really great. We used to lie on the floor and a friend of mine would read the Bible in a very loud voice and we'd curl up with laughter. And I think one of the best things is that you're walking around all the time, in the streets at night, and it's pouring with rain and you just can't stop walking. You run everywhere.

The effects of speed became central to the mod life-style. Speed produced the

'all-nighter': the Friday or Saturday night club thrash that went on till bleary-eyed breakfast-time. Speed produced the loudness, the confidence, the restlessness, the energy, the swagger. Speed produced the obsessiveness, the meticulous concern with details of dress, music, dancing or scooter-ornamentation. Speed produced the aggression, the barely-controlled 'Who-you-lookin'-at?' nastiness that sometimes erupted into violence. And speed produced the gum-chewing indifference which mod boys displayed towards mod girls, because speed suppresses the sex-drive.

After the new law came into force in 1964, the street-price of purple hearts went up from 6d to 9d. It didn't make a lot of difference.

Of course for every mod that was blocked and stuttering there were many who were too poor, nervous or out-of-touch to take anything but the over-diluted orange juice they sold in the clubs. It didn't matter. Speed set the style, and the style diffused itself from the ace faces to their retinues, then to the outer circle and finally to everyone who liked the idea of being a nice clean mod rather than a dirty greasy rocker.

Every ex-mod has his or her own litany of 'a week in the life'. Each is different, but each is amazingly rigid. Here is one:

Monday night:
 Tottenham Royal
Tuesday night:
 the Scene Club
Wednesday night:
 the Purley Orchid
Thursday night:
 Tottenham Royal
Friday night:
 the Scene Club
Saturday morning:
 shopping for clothes and records
Saturday night:
 party or club all-nighter
Sunday morning:
 Brick Lane market
Sunday afternoon:
 the Marquee Club
Sunday night:
 the Lyceum or a French film

All the itineraries accord major importance to the Scene Club in Ham Yard, Soho. This was indeed mod Mecca. Its manager in the early days was Ronan

he's so fine

O'Rahilly, the man who started Radio Caroline, and it was the first to put on a group called the High Numbers, which later became the Who.

The other thing that emerges clearly from such lists is the importance of dancing. It was practically all they ever did. Anything worked at that hard for that long becomes either very simple or very elaborate, and mod dancing became elaboration squared (except for the ones who couldn't dance and just shuffled dispiritedly from foot to foot, hour after hour after hour). Once they had exhausted the capacity of the American song-writing industry to think up silly new dance-names (the monkey, locomotion, popeye, waddle, hitch-hike, mashed potato, watusi, Madison, pony, dog, fly, funky chicken, etc.) mods were out on their own. They invented two basic steps, the *block* and the *bang*, each with myriad variations. The word to describe these dances was 'nifty'. And having mastered the intricacies of alternating heel-and-toe work, they had to look cool while doing it. The result made Highland sword-dancing look like the skinhead stomp.

While dancing, it was helpful, though not essential, to have partners, but they would probably not be spoken to (the music was too loud anyway) and their existence would be acknowledged only by the direction faced while dancing. At the end of the night the mod boys and mod girls paired up and went off as couples (or failed to), but no observer could have divined the subtle eye-signals by which the pairings had been achieved (or not).

▼ **Cathy McGowan did rather well out of being a typical teenager on television. In August 1966, she launched a record-player she'd designed herself. The adverts, inevitably, called it 'fabulous'.**

The guys were the focus of attention and the girls took a back seat. We orbited really. We orbited round their stars.

Girls were out of fashion, almost, and the guys wore the suits to impress the other guys, and they'd say 'You seen his shoes?' and 'Look at his hair', and 'What records you got?' But it was almost as if it was uncool to be seen chatting up a girl, and it was as if the roles had been reversed. The boys were getting prettier and the girls were getting plainer.

Unable to excite much of a sexual response in her pill-popping peacock beau, the mod girl would stand, uneasily clutching a big square handbag, wearing the uniform, trying to look right, being ignored, wishing she knew who the hell Howlin' Wolf was. The uniform this week might be cropped hair, a T-shirt with an initial on it (though never, of course, her *own* initial), a long grey skirt, white anklesocks and plimsolls. Or it might be a light tan mohair suit with white tights, a string of beads and clumpy Rosa Klebb shoes. The face would be blanked out with panstick and white lipstick, leaving only huge black Dusty Springfield eyes peering from beneath a Cathy McGowan fringe that she had spent all afternoon straightening by ironing it on folded newspaper (*Private Eye* was about the right thickness). The overall look was boxy, flat-chested, dowdy. She might be standing at the roadside hoping to be associated with a chrome-encrusted scooter at the

kerb (preferably the one with the cus-tomised kandy-flake panels and the meaningless initials. Mod boys were very keen on meaningless initials). If she was lucky the scooter's owner would come along, mount his throne, pat the pillion (without, of course, looking at her) and she would scramble gratefully aboard.

Almost all the mods who went to Clacton for Easter '64 went by train, but they would have preferred to go by scooter. Although a Vespa or Lambretta was a highly desirable adjunct to the mod boy's image (girls never drove scooters) it was never essential, not in the way that a motorbike became indis-pensable to the self-respecting rocker, and never to be preferred to a car.

If a mod boy did have a scooter, on the other hand, it was more than a mode of transportation: it was what anthro-pologists call a fetish-object. It might have cost him £20 down and three years' repayments, but he couldn't be seen on it until he'd spent another £50-plus on extra mirrors, lights, crash-bars, horns, mascots, mudflaps, fur trim, leopardskin seat cover and a fifteen-foot aerial with a tiger-tail (free with Esso petrol) on the end. If, loaded thus with precious metal, the machine would barely achieve thirty miles an hour, that didn't matter, because it would gen-erally be cruising in v-formation at only half that speed. If your hair got ruffled, you were going *too fast*. No wonder the rockers felt peeved. Mod scooters violated their basic beliefs about what two wheels were *for*.

Who, then, were the rockers? There is a theory that they were invented by the Press; that there was no such thing as a developed leather-and-motorbike sub-culture until it became necessary to characterise the opposition to mod, to muster Roundheads to fight the Cava-liers. It's almost true, but not quite.

Rockers were the lost patrol, the beleaguered remnants of the Teddy boy cavalry. Like mounted renegades escaped from the rock'n'roll reservation, they lurked in the country towns and villages, circled the fringes of the pale-face mod cities and rode the motor-way trails.

The rocker prototypes were Marlon Brando in *The Wild One* (a film not shown in the UK until the sixties, although it was released in the US in 1953) and Gene Vincent, after Jack Good turned him into a leather-clad hoodlum for British television. Their uni-form was a black leather jacket (possibly decorated with studs and/or painted slogans), oily jeans, motor-bike boots. Hair was worn long, greasy and quiffed.

The rocker philosophy was puritan, conservative and existentialist. They were puritan in that they disapproved of drunkenness, drug-taking and any sort of sexual sophistication or concern for fashion. They were conservative in that they thought and talked much like their working-class war-veteran fathers. They believed in the virtues of hard work, manliness and patriotism. Their musical taste was unchanging – a simple, strong attachment to no-nonsense, juke-box-shaking rock'n'roll. They were existentialist in that they built their lives around the here-and-now buzz of riding powerful bikes as fast as possible.

Rocker style was rough, tough, physical, extrovert, unreflective. They pushed and shoved and jostled each other, they jeered and spat, catcalled and farted. They waved flick-knives about in mock menace, and emptied transport café sugar bowls into one anothers' Brylcreemed hair.

▼ **Leather, goggles and a doomed gaze ... In 1940 he might have flown a Spitfire, but in 1964 he rides a motorbike.**

he's so fine

The underlying difference between mods and rockers, deeper than styles or philosophies, was a difference of aspiration. If you'd asked a mod where he was heading in the long run, he'd have talked about 'making it', becoming rich and famous, moving up through the scummy levels to the top. Perhaps Joe Lambton was the first mod. A rocker would have shrugged and said he expected to settle down, marry, have kids, live in a council house, work in a factory. That's if he survived; a lot didn't. Each time a new collecting-box appeared on the counter at the Ace or the Busy Bee, the regulars would sit round nodding their agreement that death in a quick, clean pile-up was infinitely preferable to life as a brain-damaged cabbage.

Bank Holidays were brilliant. We lived for them. We lived for Bank Holidays. You had to be on the sea front on a Bank

As mods turned into ▶ hippies, rockers mutated slowly into greasers – but even they wore headbands.

Holiday because all these boys came from mystical, magical places like London.

The place was thronging and you could have passed out with the fumes as these phalanxes of scooters went up and down the sea front. It was terribly exciting.

It was all a milling around, but somebody thought 'Oh, let's go on the pier', and nobody had any money left so they jumped over the barrier, and the guy at the barrier

panicked and called the police. Well everybody was on the pier, so the police had everybody cordoned off, and it was getting off the pier that started it. But it got a bit silly, the riots thing.

The reporter who described this little contretemps for the *Daily Express* had the imagination of a poet, the prose-style of a paperback blurb-writer and the resourcefulness common to members of his profession on slow news-days.

Last night Clacton was still flinching as violence fizzed and fizzled like a dying bonfire under the Easter Monday rain and a chill wind sweeping off a sulky sea.

More than 100 teenagers have been arrested. A whole town has come under mob rule.

I talked to crowds of mop-haired, lean-hipped, raucous kids who wheeled about the seafront in rowdy groups. They were not shy, nor ashamed of the exploits of the night before. Just excited and exhilarated. Drunk with notoriety. Anonymous. . . .

What are they trying to prove, these mods, doll-like, meticulous, blasé – and the rockers, gleaming, greasy leather-jacketed, belligerent?

Perhaps, in a childish, violent and senseless manner, that they are

he's so fine

something and someone to be reckoned with.

The reporters then were all old boys who just sat in pubs, and you used to walk in and they'd interview you and you'd tell them anything they wanted to hear, and they'd just write it down and that was it – you'd see your name in the papers.

The Press really played it up. There was hardly any bother at all at Clacton, but there was no news, so the Press had to put something in the papers and they put this sort of 'scooter riot frenzy' stuff at Clacton and made out this big mod-rocker battle thing. So after that, every Bank Holiday, they were waiting for where it was going to happen next, you see. So the scene was set, you know, and the kids would oblige.

By Whitsun, the expectation had been created (in mods, rockers, the Press, police and holiday-makers) that there would be trouble at the seaside, and so it came to pass in Brighton, Margate and Bournemouth. The violence was so thoroughly premeditated that it was not so much committed as performed.

I saw a number of fights on the beach at Brighton and it was usually something like about nine big, tough-looking rockers in leather jackets versus about 200 mods who would sort of run up to them and go 'Yah! Grrr!' and then run away. But on the whole, mods were quite small, not particularly tough guys and one-to-one the rocker would beat shit out of the guy.

What it was, in a lot of these places the whole population was rockers. I remember three of us walked into this café which we didn't know was a rockers' hangout. We just went in there and out of the back room they walked, about fifteen of the biggest guys! My bottle went, know what I mean? I thought 'Cor, bloody hell mate!' And

◄ **Thousands of mods went to Brighton for Easter 1965, and waited for the battle to begin. Police reported only a few violent incidents.**

they sort of came at us, and one of my mates who was a bit heavy said 'Leave it out, chaps. We just want to have a cup of tea. We didn't know it was your manor. We'll leave.' And as we left, of course, they felt we'd lost face and they came after us, and as we went round the corner, the rest of the firm turned up. They came after the three of us but when we got round the corner there was like twenty of our friends there, and then we was in the majority. And there was a little mish-mash there, but that got a bit overdone in the paper.

At Brighton you expected trouble and we did see some pretty horrible things. We saw a guy set alight under the pier. He had his clothes on fire, then an ambulance came and took him away. Real mods weren't interested in that sort of stuff. But by then the thing had broadened out and you'd got this loutish hooligan element involved. A lot of the true faces cut themselves off from it when that happened.

When the youths who had been arrested (who were, as is usual in these situations, not so much those who were guilty as those who were grabbed) appeared before the town magistrates, they were severely dealt with. A twenty-two-year-old from Blackheath was treated to this widely-quoted harangue from the Chairman of the Margate bench, Mr George Simpson:

It is not likely that the air of this town has ever been polluted by hordes of hooligans, male and female, such as we have seen this weekend, and of whom you are an example.

These long-haired, mentally unstable, petty little sawdust Caesars seem to find courage like rats by hunting only in packs.

The man's offence, according to the police, was that 'while running with a group of youths, he knocked into a fruit stall'. He was sentenced to three months' imprisonment.

In the end we stopped going, because everyone from all over the country used to come down. They weren't really mods, they were just looking for a fight. It got a bit silly.

By the end of 1964 the word 'mod' had acquired so many shades of meaning that it had virtually ceased to denote anything in particular. As applied to a youth 'image' it could refer to the scooter boy in his fur-trimmed anorak or to the long-haired, faintly effeminate coffee bar poseur in white trousers and a Mondrian-patterned jacket. It could mean a 'hard mod', the missing link that would eventually mutate into the 'peanut' and ultimately the skinhead, or it could mean the 'soul boy' in pork-pie hat and dark glasses. In a wider context it was merely an adjective denoting approval.

everybody's gonna be happy

'London was the hub of the world. Everybody was coming to London, the Americans, everyone, because that's where it was at. You walked down Carnaby Street on a Saturday afternoon and the whole world was in Carnaby Street. It was the place to be.'

*everybody's
gonna
be happy*

In the middle years of the sixties, British youth fell in love with its own reflection. Having been ignored in the early fifties, patronised in the late fifties and worried over in the early sixties, teenagers were now to be flattered and fawned upon in a manner which in retrospect seems quite extraordinary.

The commercial, political and cultural decision-makers (the establishment, for want of a better word), had not suddenly decided that spotty seventeen-year-olds were fab, gear and groovy. In the main, they despised them as profoundly as ever (although such was the ebullient mood of the times that they no longer felt quite so threatened by the energy of working-class youth). The difference was, in the last analysis, one of numbers.

Six years on from Abrams' *The Teenage Consumer*, the stakes had increased considerably; there were now six million teenagers in the UK, spending £1500 million a year. Commerce, having finally got its act together, was ready for them.

The record companies, who in 1964 sold over 100,000,000 discs, already knew about the teenage market; the clothing industry too had been aware of it for a while; but now there were other businessmen sniffing the breeze and working out ways to give their products – be they magazines, lampshades, cigarettes, movies, hamburgers or lipsticks – 'teen appeal'.

Suddenly there were magazines like 'Honey' and 'Rave' and terrible comics, 'Valentine' and 'Roxy'. I especially liked 'Valentine' because it had the Beatles in. After that they turned glossy and the middle pages were always a big poster of somebody like Paul McCartney or the Yardbirds or the Small Faces.

Among the first entrepreneurs to see the potential rewards of targeting the teenage market were the radio pirates. The first of them to get his station on the air was Ronan O'Rahilly. Having persuaded five City millionaires to back him, acquired a ship, a crew of discjockeys and engineers, two ten-kilowatt transmitters (£50,000 apiece) and a stack of records, it was his stroke of genius to represent himself as being, as he later put it, 'part of a revolution … against the entire forces of the establishment'.

Within weeks the station was attracting seven million regular listeners, the majority of them teenagers. A month later the second pirate, Radio Atlanta, moored itself nearby, and a month after that Screaming Lord Sutch ('National Teenage Party' candidate in a 1963 by-election – and still at it) set himself up on a disused fort in the Thames estuary and started broadcasting rock'n'roll and extracts from *Lady Chatterley's Lover*. Caroline moored a second ship off Ramsey in the Isle of Man; Radio London, the slickest operation yet, joined the airwaves, along with 'swinging' Radios City, Britain, King, Victor, England, 227, 270 and the 'easy listening' pirate, 390. There was music everywhere.

The BBC was just so square. Anything like Radio One was unthought-of. Children's Favourites! You had to listen to 'Nellie the Elephant' and all that kind of thing for five records before you got the Beatles. That was it before the pirates came along.

It would be a tiny tranny that you'd have clamped to your ear and also you'd have it under your pillow at night, and the batteries would wear down and it would get fainter and fainter, but that's what I remember. We had them all the time.

You'd wake up in the morning and the first thing you'd do would be to switch on the radio. We would bring our radios to school; if we could actually play the music in school as well, I mean, that was really something, you know. I mean, all the time music was there in the background and foreground of your life.

Garner Ted Armstrong! The Plain Truth with Garner Ted Armstrong! A crescendo of music and this terrible American voice bible-thumping …

The pirates were not merely a money-spinner for their shareholders, a pulpit for Garner Ted (whose subsidies filled pirate chests at the price of glazing many millions of teenage eyeballs) and a convenience to the listeners; they crucially altered the perception of music and its role in teenage life. Jonathan King has expressed it well:

everybody's gonna be happy

The greatest thing that the pirates did for pop music was create an atmosphere of excitement and adventure which hadn't really existed before in pop music. By doing all that out on the ocean, going up and down, struggling through absolutely enormous odds to get music to their public, the whole music took on a new sort of feeling of necessity. If somebody was really prepared to go through sheer hell just to play you a Tremeloes record, then that Tremeloes record had really to be a very important thing in your life.

I developed a devotion away from my school work to things like pop culture and pop music. It began to dominate. I let it dominate. I wanted it to dominate. It was my rebellion.

What pirate radio did for the wireless, 'Ready Steady Go!' did for television. The show had trickled unpromisingly onto the screen in August 1963, hosted by chunky Keith Fordyce in a tightly-buttoned suit, crinkly hair and a cheese-eating grin. Two subsequent smart moves saved it: the first was the elevation to presenter status of a stunningly ordinary London teenager called Cathy McGowan who spoke the same language as the audience ('smashing', 'fabulous', 'triffic') and the second was its conversion into the mods' very own shop window, a process which was reported thus in the *Daily Mail* in January 1964:

Two thousand angry teenagers charged the glass doors of Television House, Kingsway, last night after being locked out of an audition for the 'Ready, Steady, Go!' twist show.

Girls fainted and were trampled as the crowd grew more furious outside the building. Two ambulances and 100 policemen were called to stop the trouble turning into a riot.

There was a quarter-mile traffic jam and five youths were arrested and charged with obstruction.

A programme official told me: 'We never dreamed that 2000 would turn up. I don't know how the glass doors stood up to them. We were

looking for some really sharp-dressing mods for our show. We never thought there would be 2000 mods in London. Lord knows where they all came from.'

(The dancers for later shows were hand-picked from among the regulars at the Scene Club.)

Oh, 'Ready Steady Go!' I absolutely loved. Those dancers! And there was Cathy McGowan who had the hair-style of the day then, this long, straight, shaggy-dog look.

There were so many groups – the Dave Clark Five, the Animals, Herman's Hermits, hundreds and hundreds of groups. I had all the records of all these and in their own way they were all very important. Looking at them now on old tapes of 'Ready Steady Go!' you realise how alike they were in their schoolboy-ish sort of looks, the sort of innocence, the naïveté. They were all equally important because they were all part of the total picture.

▼ **Launched as 'the girl who sings in bare feet', a vaguely shocking notion at the time, Sandie Shaw took to the Swinging London dollybird image like a flamingo to water.**

63

*everybody's
gonna
be happy*

The programme was also important as a medium for introducing to British audiences the best American black artists. It would regularly feature Tamla Motown performers such as the Miracles, Marvelettes, Supremes, Four Tops, Marvin Gaye or Little Stevie Wonder, as well as soul stars like Otis Redding and James Brown and blues giants like Jimmy Witherspoon and B.B. King. It was the first pop music programme on television to book its acts according to criteria of taste rather than record sales figures. (There have been precious few since.)

By the middle of the decade, the UK's six million teenagers had acquired all the elements of their own culture. It was sharply differentiated both from 'official' mainstream culture (classical music, ballet, theatre, etc.) and from adult popular culture (pubs, bingo, ballroom dancing, most television, football, etc.). It had its own music, newspapers, magazines, dress, radio stations, television programmes, clubs, concerts, language and leaders. Admittedly, some of these elements had been kindly supplied by commercially-minded adults, but they had been demanded by the young rather than foisted upon them, and whether in it or out of it, everyone regarded the new 'youth culture' as belonging to the teenagers themselves.

It was the apparent self-sufficiency of the young, their confidence and optimism, that mesmerised the grown-ups. As well as commercial power, they were felt to have, and therefore had, considerable political influence. In January 1963, in the course of one of those hefty anatomies of British youth which *The Sunday Times* ran by the yard in those days, Godfrey Smith argued that 'Any government that permitted unemployment to persist at even today's level would be doomed, hence the speed and scale of the Government's reaction to it. The young will not know, as their fathers too often did, what it is to live indefinitely with idle hands and empty bellies.'

And magically, for as long as people believed this, it was true.

It seems even more extraordinary, seen from twenty years on, that the Prime Minister should have felt it necessary to preside at the reopening of the refurbished Cavern Club in the summer of 1966. Mr Wilson was presented with a pipe carved from a chunk of the stage on which the Beatles had played, and he made a speech. 'Now there will be those,' he declared, 'who

look down their pompous noses at pop culture. There is, of course, a tendency to decry youth or to sensationalise the actions of a small and scruffy minority who carry liberty beyond licence to dangerous and self-destructive addictions and other forms of getting kicks in the seamier purlieus of London's nightlife, a problem which, I may say, the Home Secretary is making a drive to clean up. But these people, and other delinquents, are not typical in any way of Britain's youth.'

Clearly perceiving that, as Dylan put it, their sons and their daughters were beyond their command, the grown-ups looked long and hard for reassurance that, in Pete Townshend's words, the Kids were Alright. The newspapers, rummaging selectively in the undergrowth, supplied it. Never before or since had so much space been given to announcing that there was no story.

'DARING, DEFIANT, DYNAMIC', the *Sunday People* blazoned across two broadsheet pages, 'That is Arthur Helliwell's verdict on young Britain – "THE UNKNOWN GENERATION".'

Helliwell, his trilby firmly in place, had been exploring:

... the swinging, switched-on, with-it world of young people in the UK ... a world as remote and unpredictable as Mars. A world beyond our ken. It's slick and glossy. Bold and brash. Defiant and vital.

After a few more paragraphs in this vein ('dolly girls ... superbly confident young men ... new standards of freedom and frankness ... brave new world, etc.), Helliwell came to the point:

Forget the mods and rockers. Forget the bicycle-chain gangs. Forget the lunatic fringe of unwashed pill-takers, scruffy beatniks and hairy layabouts.

We know *too* much about this over-publicised, grubby little minority; and the truth is that they are outnumbered more than ten to one by the normal, decent young people of Britain. They don't take drugs. They don't smoke reefers or get drunk. They don't indulge in wild sexual orgies. But they do live tremendously exciting lives at a breathless, breakneck pace that completely baffles their perplexed and confused mothers and fathers ... Whatever activity they engage in, from dancing until dawn to ten pin bowling or party-going, they plunge into it with a tremendous and dynamic zest.

Young people were worshipped by the Press. Everybody was in awe of young people, you know.

Youngsters had got hold of some kind of arcane knowledge that the oldsters really wanted to get at.

Lurking behind this fascination with zestful ten pin bowling was an unhealthy amount of prurient sexual envy. When the grown-ups weren't banging on about all the drugs that were or were not being taken and checking the cleanliness of teenage fingernails to make sure they weren't attached to a member of the 'grubby little minority', they were creeping about, flashlights at the ready, in search of TEENAGE SEX.

We used to have a system of numbers — number one, holding hands, number two, a kiss on the lips, and so on up to number ten. But I never knew anyone who got to number ten. My mother threatened that if I ever got pregnant she'd jump off the end of Bournemouth pier, and I believed her.

I'd never been a teenager before, and of course every generation thinks they've discovered sex and that the previous generation didn't do it, but maybe in our case it was a little bit true. We were having contact with the opposite sex in a much freer way than our parents, and I suppose they must have been terrified. I can remember my mother saying 'Well dear, you know what's right and wrong.' That's all she would say, and I actually felt that I didn't know, that I had to work it out as I went along. My friends and I had to work out in a very painful way whether certain activities were or were not acceptable.

everybody's gonna be happy

▼ January 1967, and at the UFO Club the dancing is getting freakier all the time.

▼ Inside the 'Hung On You' boutique, with its Beardsley-print decor, London's gilded youth reflects on its own importance.

everybody's gonna be happy

We used to go to other people's houses and have evenings in, and the parents would go out, and then we would pair off and disappear into dark corners while somebody was detailed to keep watch. Then it was 'Parents coming!' and the lights would go on and we'd emerge from our corners ... It wasn't all innocence.

I can remember having boyfriends and going to the cinema with them, and you instantly get into a situation where you've got to make the rules. The poor boy is obviously trying it out as well, and you're having to decide what you're going to let him do. I remember the battles in the stalls and the terrible feelings of guilt afterwards – should I have let him touch me there? It wasn't until later that I talked to other girls and we discovered what we'd all been up to and the sweaty encounters we'd all had.

The very word 'teenager' conjures up horror images of pop fans screaming at airports, gangs roaming the streets and long-haired rebels being rude to their headmasters – and some of the older generation react to them with an automatic shudder. The drug-taking, bottle-throwing few get front page publicity, while the sound majority are forgotten – if only because 'Many Thousands Pass A-Levels' makes a hopeless headline.

The words above were not those of Arthur Helliwell again. This was the official report of the Latey Committee on the Age of Majority which, in July 1967, recommended that eighteen-year-olds should be given the vote. Meanwhile the provision for higher education was being vastly expanded, the school-leaving age was being raised to sixteen and the minimum age for being sent to prison had gone up to seventeen. A society that declared itself in favour of youth was putting its money where its mouth was.

Too much adulation is probably not good for the immature. The cries of 'Blasphemy!' which erupted when John Lennon remarked that the Beatles were now 'bigger than Jesus' obscured the real point: the Beatles were now becoming thoroughly big-headed, and no wonder. The bumblebee of youth cul-

ture had flown because it didn't know it couldn't. Now it was being told that it could loop-the-loop backwards. The more seriously it took itself, the sillier it got.

Time magazine (which nominated as its Man of the Year for 1966 'the man or woman of twenty-five and under') must bear part of the blame for creating the myth of Swinging London. In April that year it announced:

In a decade dominated by youth, London has burst into bloom. It swings; it is the scene. This spring, as never before in modern times, London is switched on. Ancient elegance and new opulence are all tangled up in a dazzling blur of op and pop. The city is alive with birds (girls) and beatles, buzzing with minicars and telly stars, pulsing with half a dozen separate veins of excitement ... Discs by the thousand spin in a widening orbit of discotheques, and elegant saloons have become gambling parlours. In a once sedate world of faded splendour, everything new, uninhibited and kinky is blooming at the top of London life.

This tourist brochure prose, which gushed into newspapers, magazines (especially the Sunday supplements) and books such as *Len Deighton's London Dossier*, brought thousands of eager youngsters swarming into the capital to stake their own claims on the golden pavements.

The clothes! Bibas' in Kensington High Street! We just used to flock down there. Vidal Sassoon! To have a Vidal Sassoon hair-cut in his salon in Bond Street! You couldn't aim any higher. And it was all in London. Nothing was better in America. Nothing was better in Europe. It was London it was happening in and to be part of it was so fabulous. You were caught up in it.

I can remember having skirts which I turned up and turned up and turned up. They got shorter and shorter.

The skirts were like pelmets. They were hardly worth having really.

And there were just racks with dresses on, no changing rooms. Girls were stripping off and trying on these things, fighting over them. It was all spend, spend, spend . . .

By the end of 1966 the pattern of teenage spending had changed significantly. The main trend had been away from record-buying and towards clothes-buying. Girls now spent a third of their income on clothes, almost as much as they spent on holidays, records, meals and magazines put together. It was predicted that within twelve months the boys would be spending even more on their clothes than the girls.

The cycle of supply and demand was spinning faster, but no-one knew which was pushing and which was pulling. Were the boutique owners following where the teenagers led, or were they taking their young customers for a fast and lucrative ride? John Stephen, the most influential of the Carnaby Street pants-peddlers, gave a radio interview in August 1964 which ventured a more sophisticated analysis:

Young people are the trendsetters. Why are they trendsetters? Lots of them don't have a lot of money and consequently, what they have already bought they attempt to adapt, they attempt to change the style and from this we get new trends which we follow up in our shops.

We watch the young people because we're with-it and we're young, you know . . . I go round our shops and I watch these young people trying on goods and from this I get an idea of what they want without them actually knowing what they want. In one instance, I've noticed that young lads over the last year have been putting on those little square jackets and sort of pulling them down at the back. So this tells me something: it tells me they want the jackets a bit longer. So consequently, the following season, the jackets are a bit longer.

Partly because fashion was led by pop stars who had to be extreme to be noticed, and partly because in an accelerating spiral of outrageousness the short-cut to being ultra-fashionable was to go a little, or even a lot, further than anyone went last week, the pattern of change in styles was a steady progress towards ever-wilder excess. That was why skirts got shorter, shirts got louder, trousers tighter, blouses more transparent, why T-shirts started to scream slogans and men wore beads and lipstick. The durability of clothes was no longer a consideration; all that mattered was impact.

Everything was plastic. We wore plastic clothes, plastic boots, plastic macs, plastic dresses; all disposable: easy come, easy go.

There were some extraordinary things. I had a paper dress with sort of twirly patterns on it, and it was orange and pink. It was all wear it today, throw it away next week.

▼ **John Stephen and Diana Harris, with a mini-dress to match the door-panels on the mini-car.**

everybody's gonna be happy

Mr Wilfred Dawes, Headmaster of a secondary school in Derbyshire, was quoted in the papers as saying that the Prices and Incomes Board should act to limit teenage wages.

They have become the cosseted darlings of competing employers, wooed by them at every turn. It is one of the root causes of much of the indiscipline rampant in the more irresponsible sections of that age group. The ridiculously high wages offered to teenagers in industry are gravely damaging their characters and enticing them away from worthwhile careers.

We absolutely came in on the crest of a wave. We were it. We were the welfare generation, we had orange juice when we were babies, we grew big and strong and taller and brighter. The world was your oyster. You knew it was there for the asking. Nobody ever questioned that you would get a job. Mind you, being female, there was also very strongly the feeling that you wouldn't really be wanting to get a job; what you'd really be wanting was to get a husband. But he would have a jolly good job.

There were two levels going on all the time in the sixties. One was the popular consumption, this is what you'll really love, churn it out of the sausage machine, headlines in the 'Daily Mirror' blah blah, which people like us, who came through that, saw for what it was. And if people think that's what we were doing in the sixties they're wrong, because underneath all that there was something else going on. It was a kind of fundamental feeling that you could have what you wanted. It was kicking open all the doors simultaneously and inviting you to walk through into any of the rooms that was so exciting. And all that razzmatazz about Beatlemania and miniskirts and London being the swinging place to be, you know, I thought that was so much hoo-ha, like all the hoo-ha that's always going on, because people like to sell their Mars Bars, don't they?

hello, i love you

'We simply, as the expression of the time went, "let it all hang out", and we took our clothes off and jiggled the extremities of our anatomies around for the cameramen who were hanging about, and danced for three days non-stop.'

hello, i love you

One of the favourite adjectives of the enthusiasts for the cult of youth was 'classless' and it bears examination. Much was made of the humble origins of such aristocrats of youth culture as the Beatles, David Bailey, Terence Stamp, Michael Caine, Sandie Shaw and Twiggy, but one swallow does not make a summer and a handful of actors, photographers, models and singers do not make a class revolution. For every Paul McCartney there was a Jane Asher, for every Mick Jagger a Marianne Faithfull, and for every Mary Quant an Alexander Plunket-Greene. Again, the myth was what mattered; because people thought class was no bar to advancement, it did (for a while and within a limited range of professions) become less important.

Times were changing because the class system was changing such a lot and whoever you were you could make it big. You could come from a working-class home, the poorest of the poor, and you could be a star very, very quickly, as people like Twiggy proved.

It became fashionable to be working class. I'm sure everybody remembers the fact that even the aristocracy started speaking with cockney accents and it was very, very fashionable to be a working-class boy made good and it was terribly unfashionable to be posh. And we all used to put on accents. We stopped talking nicely and started speaking just slightly wrong.

The accent that emerged as a result of this self-conscious vowel-shifting was neither public school nor proletarian but a hybrid drawl with a hint of the trans-atlantic. It was diffused through the influence of pirate disc-jockeys and achieved its quintessence in the laid-back mumblings of Mick Jagger. Accused by a radio interviewer of 'trying to project the image that the Rolling Stones are a lot of inarticulate yobbos' he replied in as yobbish a voice as he could manage:

We don't really try and project any-thing. People who write the articles really know what they want more or less and so they write 'Oh, the Rolling Stones are a load of yobs'

and everyone is very prepared to be-lieve it. I really don't care whether they think we're a load of yobs or not. I don't mind what they think about me.

Pop stars like Jagger were at least partly responsible for establishing the late-sixties convention that to be inarticulate was not necessarily to be stupid; it was, on the contrary, evidence that one's thoughts were too deep for words; or that one's life was so different, exciting and trendy that one had no point of contact with one's interlocutor; or that one was out of one's skull on dope; or all three.

As we have seen, until the mid-sixties, the middle-class grammar-school-and-university tradition was not only outside commercial pop culture but was deeply suspicious of it. Alongside the Mozart and Sibelius in the record rack might be a Joan Baez LP or even 'Freewheelin' Bob Dylan', but it was quite impossible to pronounce the words Gerry and the Pacemakers with-out an involuntary curling of the lip.

The next generation along, hitting their teens in '63 or '64, were a good deal less sniffy about the whole thing. Because youth culture was being taken seriously by *The Times* and the *Guardian* (and because it was taking *itself* ever more seriously), an interest in it was ceasing to be intellectually disreputable.

When the Animals recorded a couple of songs from the first Bob Dylan LP, supplying a rock backing where Dylan had strummed acoustic guitar, a taboo was broken. The Byrds' folk-rock version of 'Mr Tambourine Man' went to number one in the summer of 1965 and Dylan himself promptly hired a rock group to accompany his increasingly surrealistic lyrics. There were those who hissed and shouted 'Judas!' when he brought his band on tour, but for every unreconstructed folknik he alienated, he recruited two or three devotees to his new, intellectually respectable brand of rock'n'roll.

Dylan's arrival, I mean it was a great arrival because we'd been listening to Dylan from the early sixties and I was fantastically impressed with his stuff and when he electrified I was made up. I mean a lot of the folkies threw up their hands in horror, didn't they? Gave him this

terrible time. But of course he was absolutely great electric.

I was very disappointed when he went electric because I felt he had sold out to commercialism.

The Beatles, meanwhile, were moving away from the Merseybeat simplicities of 'She Loves You' (yeah, yeah, yeah) and venturing further with each LP in the direction of the sort of lyrics that would ring the bell with the A-level Eng. Lit. crowd.

They say that Bobby Dylan gave John Lennon his first joint, and it's probably true, and there's a kind of mythological meaning to that. He also liberated John Lennon to write pop songs in the style of the funny little poems he'd been writing since he was five or six or seven years old. You know, John Lennon didn't think you could do that in rock'n'roll songs and Bob Dylan showed people that you could just describe the dream, that it was all right. In fact that's really what the music was all about! He was moving to meet the Beatles and the Beatles were moving to meet him, and the result really was the second-stage flowering of the sixties.

In May 1966 the Beatles gave up live performance; from now on they would be seen on film and television and heard on record, and that would be all. It was symptomatic of an important change in the way pop music was used. Clubs were turning from live groups to discotheques; concerts were becoming bigger, louder, more expensive and less frequent; the Dansette was giving way to the stereo 'hi-fi' and the sales of LPs were increasing at the expense of singles. Moreover, the two markets were growing apart; singles now were aimed at the teenyboppers on the one hand or the mums'n'dads on the other, while the teenagers who were serious about music bought the albums (which now began to include the tracks available as singles). In 1966, the best-selling singles were by Jim Reeves, Frank Sinatra, Herb Alpert and Dave Dee, Dozy, Beaky, Mick and Tich; the best-selling albums were by the Beach Boys, the Beatles, the Walker Brothers and the Rolling Stones. (The following year, the top three best-

selling singles were *all* by Englebert Humperdinck.)

Pop's new-found pretensions grew out of a cross-fertilisation with the cultural avant-garde which had been blossoming during the early sixties. Once the two had interbred, it became a matter of little consequence whether people flocked to Ravi Shankar concerts because of a fascination with Indian classical music, or because George Harrison and Brian Jones had taken up the sitar. It was a matter of even less consequence whether they bought the Beatles' or the Stones' records because of the sitar or in spite of it. Peter Blake painted portraits of the Beatles and some art buffs said 'Who?' and a lot more Beatles fans said 'Who?', but by and by everybody found out so that was all right. People with names like Ralph Ortiz and Gustav Metzger had been creating sculpture by tearing up armchairs and pianos, so when the Who smashed their equipment on stage this was not zonked-out mods on the rampage, this was Autodestructive Art (especially after Jeff Beck did the same thing in Antonioni's *Blow Up*). Then the Move cottoned on to the idea and started hacking up television sets and cardboard cut-outs of Harold Wilson and one started to wonder.

*hello,
i love you*

▼ **Having launched surrealist rock, Bob Dylan broke his neck in a motorbike crash in July 1966 and disappeared for eighteen months, neatly avoiding the flower-power silly season.**

hello, i love you

In 1965, the poet Adrian Henri wrote:

Paul McCartney Gustav Mahler
Alfred Jarry John Coltrane
Charlie Mingus Claude Debussy
Wordsworth Monet Bach and Blake

Charlie Parker Pierre Bonnard
Leonardo Bessie Smith
Fidel Castro Jackson Pollock
Gandhi Milton Munch and Berg

Belà Bartók Henri Rousseau
Rauschenberg and Jasper Johns
Lukas Cranach Shostakovitch
Kropotkin Ringo George and John

(It goes on for another ten stanzas but you get the idea.) 'In 1960', says Jeff Nuttall in *Bomb Culture*, 'this poem ... would have been unthinkable. By 1965, such a poem was inevitable.'

The most influential record of the sixties was probably 'Sergeant Pepper's Lonely Hearts Club Band' released by the Beatles in 1967; a continuous, thematically-structured song-cycle featuring brass band, symphony orchestra, sitar, wacky sound effects, obscure lyrics and some good tunes.

▼ Peter Blake's cover for 'Sergeant Pepper' posed the Beatles in military garb among a montage of their alleged influences, from Marlon Brando to Karl Marx, W.C. Fields to Oscar Wilde.

Sergeant Pepper was the first time I really realised how powerful music could be. I remember listening to it and just being knocked out by it. I played the whole album through and thought 'My God!' I know people say music can change your life and I think it did in a way, because I thought 'This is what I want to be a part of. I want to be involved in this.'

It was strange. You found that there was other music behind it. You were hearing secret harmonies I suppose, echoes of something else.

It wasn't just an LP, it was a complete experience!

You actually had to listen to the words and the words were compelling. They were about something. It was much more intelligent, let's put it like that.

Sergeant Pepper reached the middle-class record-racks that even Joan Baez had failed to penetrate. It also had a powerfully corrupting effect on rock'n'roll.

When Procol Harum sang about picking flowers on the seashore to the sound of a trumpet voluntary and a grand piano (on a record entitled 'Magdalene My Regal Zonophone'), the Beatles were to blame.

Allen Ginsberg came to Liverpool the year after the Beatles left for good and declared it 'the centre of consciousness of the human universe'. Back in San Francisco in the summer of 1965, he told 1200 people at a poetry conference that the 'Liverpool minstrels' were leading a 'revolution of the psyche'. Luria Castell, one of the organisers of the first big rock'n'roll dances in San Francisco (who had previously been living in a tree in Mexico), announced her intention of making San Francisco 'the American Liverpool' because, unlike New York or Los Angeles, it was 'a pleasure city'.

'Basically', she said, 'we want to meet people and have a good time and not be dishonest and have a profitable thing going on.' Thus was hippiedom born of the union of idealism and bull-shit.

Dazzled by the proposition that London was the swinging centre of the human universe, British teenagers were slow to look westward and notice what was going on. The artistic avant-garde knew about Ken Kesey's Acid Trips and Timothy 'Turn-on-tune-in-drop-out' Leary, but for the vast majority, whose centre of artistic inspiration was the record counter at Boots, precious little percolated through. One or two Californian groups made an impression: the Lovin' Spoonful, a latter-day skiffle group (Americans called them jug bands), had

a summery hit or two, and the Beach Boys were coming over all fey and tinkly, but it wasn't until 1967 and the 'summer of love' that fully-fledged, head-to-toe, Frisco-model hippies made their appearance on British pavements. They had a hard time getting noticed, because teenage style had already become a seven-days-a-week fancy dress parade.

(In September 1966 an eighteen-year-old from Muswell Hill had been hauled before the magistrates, charged 'that not being a person in Her Majesty's military forces, he did wear part of the uniform of the Scots Guards without Her Majesty's permission'. What with the blue jeans and the long hair, it was hardly a serious attempt at impersonating a soldier, and he was conditionally discharged.)

Like everything else at the time, the way the kids dressed was subjected to intellectual analysis. It became a 'statement'. An earnest young art student told a BBC interviewer (in a programme called 'I Suppose They Are Human?'):

Clothes play, to me, a very important part, in that they reflect one's character. At the moment I'm wearing a purple scarf round my neck without a shirt. One, it keeps my neck warm, but apart from that it's just unusual and people do look at you, it boosts your ego, you like it. Your tie's pink and your trousers are pink too, *and they don't wear pink trousers!*

This effeminate late-mod style merged with other influences: Indian or Arabian 'ethnic'; scruffy cowboy (the spaghetti western was big at the time); fairy-tale; American Indian (buckskin, feathers, moccasins), rural peasant; Beardsley print and Hell's Angel. But the strongest influence on the hippie look was the most direct: television and magazine pictures of the 'freaks' on the streets of Haight Ashbury, San Francisco.

Strangely enough, I think what got me interested in being a hippie was an article that I read in the 'Readers' Digest' about the hippies who lived in Haight Ashbury. It depicted them as very irresponsible people who had dropped out of awfully good homes to go and look scruffy and take drugs and bring up children in appalling conditions. So what the 'Readers' Digest' was doing was trying to make all its readers believe how irresponsible and awful these people were, and of course I admired them and I wanted to be the first in our village to do it.

I used to go around in my grandfather's cut-down velvet dressing gown, which I made into a jacket, and ratty old jeans and fifty million beads.

A yellow kaftan, a second-hand fur coat, beads, a headband which had 'ACID' written on it. (I'd never taken acid at the time. I just knew that was part of looking it.)

Everyone was wearing Indian print things, mostly bedspreads. I had one that was a beautiful pink and I used to paint myself and I always used to have bare feet. Everyone had long hair then, and I had a friend who had a pet water-snake. I used to put it in my hair and let it crawl about on my head just so people would do a double take when I walked by. And we were very silly: we did all sorts of things, like picking the flowers in the Municipal Gardens and handing them to people just for fun.

A bemused pet-shop wholesaler confessed in September 1967 that he could no longer attribute the sales boom in budgie-bells to a vast increase in the budgie birth-rate. He was selling 300 gross a week in the Birmingham area alone, and doing very nicely too with a line of ornamental cat collars at thirty bob a time. He put it down to the fact that 'these happy people like pretty things'.

For a significant proportion of the beautiful people, dressing up in beads and bells was all that hippiedom was about, particularly in the early days. Pressed for the philosophical implications of the headband and the sandal, they might have replied 'Peace and love', but all that meant in practical terms was that they didn't actually thump anybody.

I wasn't a hippie, I simply looked like one. I just had the clothes, but I wasn't behaving as a hippie in any way because I was going back to a semi-detached house with a car parked outside it, and Monday to Friday I was going to a private girls' school.

hello,
i love you

I think everybody wanted to try this dropping-out thing, but very few had the nerve. You operated within your local circle and you were just sufficiently weird in the local circle; that was enough, certainly for most people.

For the intellectual minority, looking weird was by no means enough. There had to be a catechism. It is too cynical to suggest that this too was bought off the peg with the psychedelic shirts and the kaftans. It did articulate a genuinely-felt revulsion against the rampant materialism of the E-type Jaguar culture.

You know, when you're sixteen you think you know it all. You can look at the world and see ever so clearly what's wrong with it. And in a sense you do know it all. It's the compromises you make as you get older, the fact that life starts to get complicated, that makes you feel wiser. All that's happened is you've lost the big picture.

We didn't half sit around and talk a lot at that stage. Whereas before, talking was actually taboo, girls and boys were decorative and you stood round eyeing each other up: now in this new age, you had to prove yourself by testing out your ideas.

(This has to be qualified with the observation that it was the height of bad manners for any hippie to disagree openly with any other hippie about anything. Hippie conversation therefore proceeded from the premise that everyone felt the same, and explored ways in which any given range of opinions might all be said to be equally valid.)

You'd look around you and it would be sterile, boring, numbing nonsense most of the time. But we, this great army of young people across the world, we could change it. The reasons why life wasn't very good were because of school, church, authority, all those things. Get rid of those and let us just be natural, you know, let people be themselves, and you'd have quite a different world.

I remember going with a group of friends to a pub in Chalk Farm and sitting down and writing out a declaration on a toilet roll, which was the only paper that was

available, and it was all about joy. It was all about joy and hope and that being the antidote to the greyness.

I remember standing in Oxford Circus and saying 'Ten years from now there'll be sheep grazing here'. And I believed it.

You know the line, never trust anyone over thirty. There was very much that. You thought 'What's wrong with the older generation? They're all strung up, following false values, and they're not really doing what they want to do, whereas we're doing everything that we want to do. We are being ourselves in a way that our parents could never understand. And that's why the future looks so hopeful, because of course there'll be more and more of us, all following our own natural, good instincts'.

The philosophy was articulated at much greater length, but along essentially those lines, in an editorial in the *International Times* in March 1967:

It is essentially an inner-directed movement. Those who are involved in it share a common viewpoint, a new way of looking at things, rather than a credo, dogma or ideology. This can never be suppressed by force or Law: you cannot imprison consciousness. No matter how many raids and arrests the police make on whatever pretence, there can be no final bust because the revolution has taken place *within the minds* of the young... There are no leaders: each individual follows his inner voice in the most honest way possible ... The new movement is essentially optimistic. It has a happy view of man and his potential, based mainly on his creativity. The weapons are love and creativity, wild new clothes fashions, strange new music sounds...

The new movement is slowly, carelessly, constructing an alternative society. It is international, inter-racial, equisexual, with ease. It operates on different conceptions of time and space. The world of the future may have no clocks.

*hello,
i love you*

When Tom McGrath wrote this, the circulation of *International Times* was a mere 12,000. The 'underground' consisted of a nucleus of arty dreamers drifting between the Indica bookshop, the Jeanetta Cochrane Theatre and the UFO nightclub. The impact of all this on the wider world was achieved through the 'overground' media, through radio, television, newspapers and magazines. The phenomenon was reported to the populace in the tones of amused bafflement which conditioned the hippie image from the outset: these people were *weird*.

In August 1967, for example, we were told about 'love-ins'. There was a 'love-in' at Hay Tor. The man from the 'Today' programme asked questions like 'Does your mother know you're here?' and 'Do you believe in free love?' and 'Why have you brought the blanket?' He concluded that 'there were half a dozen boys to every girl, and I think they'd probably gone up there out of curiosity ... What did they do? Nothing as far as I could see but stand or sit around to show off their fancy dresses.'

When the Duke of Bedford allowed the grounds of Woburn Abbey to be used for a 'Festival of the Flower Children' (featuring the Kinks, Jeff Beck, the Bee Gees, the Alan Price Set and others), he was cross-examined by a radio reporter who asked:

−Do you think this is the sort of thing that should go on in a gracious and beautiful setting like Woburn?
−Well these are people who, as I understand it, believe in peace and love and beauty.
−You don't think that's a little bit irresponsible? This could turn into an orgy of sorts. One of the papers this morning talks in terms of a hundred thousand people.
−What do you mean by an 'orgy'?
−Well, shall we say of sex and drugs at the least. Drugs being peddled right here in your own front garden ...

Perhaps to the disappointment of some, the orgy of the hundred thousand dope-crazed sex-fiends failed to materialise.

I was there as well, sort of lying on the grass being rather 'cool, man', 'laid back', but I knew it was a game. Part of me was saying, this is all just phoney, it's for show, it's still just everybody following fashions.

The most influential disseminator of hippie modes and tastes was probably the pirate disc-jockey John Peel, who was already engaged in his life's work of breaking down musical barriers, playing everything from Mongolian bagpipe music to Pink Floyd, on a late-night show called 'The Perfumed Garden'. He spoke differently in those days, his voice drifting out of the tranny in a gentle, zonked monotone, and he said things like:

That really is actually a magic record ... It's one of those things that you look at it on the turntable like you were expecting it to drift away and disappear, and it's so beautiful ... I went up during the other record to have a look at the night, which incidentally is very beautiful, so if you're anywhere near a window, go out and look at it, breathe, and perhaps yell 'I love you!' into the night ...

▼ **John Peel before the Fall (October 1968).**

Public concern about teenagers and drugs had been growing throughout the middle years of the decade and the growth in the figures for arrests and convictions has therefore to be interpreted with caution; in part it does reflect an increase in drug use, but it also reflects an increase in police activity inspired by the new policy of controlling the misuse of amphetamines.

hello,
i love you

Convictions for possession of marijuana almost doubled (to 1119) between 1965 and 1966, then doubled again in 1967 and increased more slowly in the following couple of years. Equally significantly, the proportions of white and 'coloured' people arrested shifted: in 1963, a majority had been West Indian immigrants; by 1967, three-quarters were white, and two-thirds under twenty-five. It is of course impossible to say what proportion of the pot-smokers ended up in court in any given year, but the Wootton Report in 1968 conservatively estimated that as many as 300,000 people in Britain had used marijuana.

The move from speed to dope, or to put it in more technically, from amphetamines to hallucinogens, altered the character of youth culture. As Jeff Nuttall puts it: 'LSD and pot created an atmosphere of harmony and inventiveness, whereas amphetamine and alcohol, at the old mod clubs, created an atmosphere of sourness, scepticism, alienation and aggression.'

Whereas we now know that the Beatles grabbed a crafty toke in the lavatory at Buckingham Palace when they went to get their MBEs, the crucial link in the public mind between rock'n'roll and drugs was forged by the Rolling Stones. In February 1967, the police raided Keith Richard's home and charged him and Mick Jagger with drug offences. In May they pounced on Brian Jones. Even the Editor of *The Times* considered that the sentence of three months' imprisonment handed down to Jagger for possession of four amphet-

amine pills, which he had bought quite legally in Italy, was excessive. In a leader entitled 'Who Breaks a Butterfly on a Wheel?' he voiced the suspicion that 'In this case Mr Jagger received a more severe sentence than would have been thought proper for any purely anonymous young man.' The Appeal court reduced the sentence to conditional discharge.

When Jagger was done for drugs, you felt a generation was on trial and all this sort of thing.

Everybody started to talk about drugs. The whisper was that the Beatles took LSD and the thing was to go on trips and then you could have amazing experiences, but I don't actually know anybody who took LSD then. We just used to think it would be rather glamorous to do so.

And that's when we started sitting on floors in smoke-filled rooms, talking about war and love and stuff like that. Of course we had no idea of what we were talking about, but it seemed jolly good at the time.

LSD – *d*-lysergic acid diethylamide 25 – is a synthetic drug first produced in 1938 and not made illegal in the US or the UK until 1965. Its effects are similar to, but more intense than, those of mescalin, which were described by Aldous Huxley in the much-discussed semi-mystical treatise *The Doors of Perception*. Acid became the sacrament of hippiedom. Timothy Leary and his acolytes used it reverentially to explore their psyches in upstate New York; Ken Kesey and his Merry Pranksters sprinkled it into the orange-juice at San Francisco freak-outs; Allen Ginsberg advocated that every man, woman and child in America try LSD at least once.

The editor of *International Times*, Tom McGrath, when asked on the radio why his paper refused to condemn the drug as dangerous, said:

What we are merely concerned to say is that for many people the drug has proved not to be dangerous, but in fact extremely beneficial, to the extent that, say, in my own case, LSD could be said to form an integral part of my life. It is in fact a part of my religion, and what I'm concerned to

▼ **Sharing a bath-time spliff with a couple of chums: Mick Jagger in a scene from 'Performance' (filmed in 1969, released 1971). He played, convincingly, a decadent rock star.**

say on my own behalf is that I should be free to take LSD, that I do myself no harm with it and do myself only good, without hindrance by the Law ... The great thing about the God that I've discovered under LSD is that he's a hip God who approves of sexuality and human pleasure. He's not the kind of God that you force down someone else's throat.

I spent twelve hours in a Disney cartoon, just watching capering colours flickering across my vision and trying to move without offending people, which isn't easy when you're that far out of it.

I remember the first one I took, going into Sefton Park and spending four hours having this unspeakably beautiful encounter with the ducks and the sunset by the lake, and returning to this guy's house and he said to me 'Are you all right?' and I said 'All right? Yeah! You ought to see the park today, it looks absolutely fantastic. The ducks!' and he said 'Could you do me a favour? Fill in this pools coupon. Look, I think you've got it right. Just put eight X's on this piece of paper. We're gonna win you know.' I said 'We've already won! You know? There IS nothing to win!' And I just couldn't understand what he was after. It was down there in the park. It was all freely available. What did he want to win?

The difference between the hippies' attitude to drugs and that of, say, the mods is that, whereas the mods had considered their illicit indulgences naughty but nice, the hippies were quite incredibly self-righteous about the whole thing. They felt, with the arrogance of the middle classes from which they came, that the police had no cause to go poking their noses into other people's private pleasures. Even parents and teachers should mind their own business. A fifteen-year-old, expelled from St. Paul's School for smoking cannabis, wrote to *Oz* magazine in aggrieved tones:

A witch-hunt is starting throughout the country for schoolboy heads, and before it does, let's try and get teacher's sense of proportions right.

Hash smoking is now a widespread social habit, almost in the same class as whisky and soda ... If people are being expelled from schools throughout the country, with a good chance of their careers being ruined, for a misdemeanour for which by law they would probably receive a penalty comparable to that for pulling the alarm cord on a train, it has got to stop somewhere.

Teenagers have always had the ability to believe both that the system is so unjust that nothing should surprise us, and that they have personally been quite astonishingly persecuted, but no generation voiced both opinions more loudly than the hippies.

One of the effects of LSD is to produce a condition called synaesthesia, in which sounds are perceived as colours and shapes, while sensations of touch are confused with tastes and smells. The concept of 'sensory overload' was developed in an attempt to reproduce this experience by non-chemical means. The idea was that, by bombarding the brain with loud and peculiar music, incense, wild dancing and light shows, it was possible to 'freak out', achieving a state of mystical, unthinking bliss. (In this endeavour a little dope too would not come amiss, but it would be the icing on the cake.)

'Psychedelic music', which was intended to produce just such an effect, was very different from the pop songs that were played on the radio. Performed at the UFO club in Tottenham Court Road by groups like Pink Floyd and the Soft Machine, it struck the untutored ear as a cacophanous, atonal racket that went on and on for hours. A projector connected to the sound system played coloured abstract images onto the musicians and the screen behind them, exploding, re-forming and throbbing to the irregular beat. It was music, as one critic put it, that was bad for your eyes. At its most extreme, the sound was meaningless away from the druggy atmosphere of the club, but it created musical clichés which found their way into the wider world of records and radio. Songs got longer, guitars screeched and stuttered a good deal, singers intoned and wailed: it was difficult music to become fond of, and its impact

*hello,
i love you*

in the album charts, let alone the singles charts, was minimal. But it was the sound of the time and the seed of the future.

When people say there's a sixties sound in music, what they're talking about is something that aims for where the imagination wants to fly. There's a sound, you know? I mean it's a musical trick, it's a recording trick, but there's a soaring noise that you can make on a record and it was a sixties sound because somehow it empathised with the spirit of the day which said 'We can go any place!'

And they did. Hippies took the beatnik notion of life on the road and extended it to its logical conclusion which is that 'the road goes on forever'. Deeply opposed to western materialism, they looked to the east, whence came weird music, pretty print fabrics and hash of fabled cheapness and potency. By dozens, by hundreds and eventually by thousands, they set off on the golden road to Samarkand.

You travelled. I mean, I went to Turkey. I bought an Afghan coat and you can imagine the kudos when somebody asks you where you got your coat and you said 'Well in Istanbul.' So you travelled overland, you got robbed by people in Yugoslavia whilst you were sleeping in the van, so you had to sleep by the side of the road for the next

two weeks of your holiday, but it was great. That's what made the holiday.

I felt when I travelled to the east that I was seeing life for the first time. When I crossed the Bosphorus and first saw Asia, you know, I felt that someone had turned up the colour knob on life, that I'd watched it in black and white all my life. It was like coming to the edge of a cliff, looking over and seeing a whole other civilisation going on that nobody had ever told you about. It was that *that you wanted access to: it wasn't to become an Indian prince, it was to find out what England was that I went to India. It was such a deep learning experience, not about the east but about the west.*

The impact of the lost tribes of western teen on the innocent cultures they invaded has been well documented. It was not entirely benign. Western society could afford a few parasites, whereas India or Nepal could not.

You can holiday into any culture. Being in a Hindu society in a small village in India is a reasonably pleasant experience: it's living in it for twenty years that's the tough part.

The ultimate achievement was to have got to the Mecca, to have got to Katmandu, to have spent some time there taking all the drugs that nature could throw at you and

A child of the ▶ universe freaks out to Hawkwind at the Richmond Pop Festival.

make it home again without having died en route. Then you could talk about it to other people who had been to Katmandu. It was the done thing, partly because you could take drugs in huge quantities in great ease and comfort for very low cost, partly for the exploration of new spiritual and religious values that were fashionable at the time, which I personally wasn't into at all.

The Maharishi Mahesh Yogi, known in *Private Eye* as the Veririchi Lotsamoney Yogi Bear (and more widely as the Giggling Guru), was only one of many sixties enthusiasms which it is now polite not to remind people they were into, but at his peak in 1967 he put together such a collection of Beatles and Stones and their girlfriends as any promoter would have given his right arm to assemble, and whisked them off to India to learn the secrets of Transcendental Meditation.

In fact, what he said, if you look back on it, was just a series of clichés that you can't really argue with, and very vacuous clichés at that.

There were a few hippies who found what they were looking for in eastern philosophy and religion. Some joined Tibetan monasteries; some are still there. But for most of those who dabbled in the ancient wisdoms of the mystic Orient, what you couldn't learn in a weekend probably wasn't worth knowing. Or as *Oz* 12 put it:

This is a fun and games *Oz*. The pull-out sheets are based on the Great Buddhist Liberation, or method of realising Nirvana by knowing the mind. Three out of the four poster-sides represent three out of the four truths which comprise Buddhism. The fourth side – and thus the fourth truth – had to be dropped because of extra advertising.

It was like a kaleidoscope, it was so brightly-coloured, and then it started to crystallise and some people chose the religious side of it and started wearing saffron robes and chanting and all that stuff, and some people became very politically aware. A lot of my friends
became either raving Marxists or raving orange people, and both of them were raving. I remember always being very suspicious of that.

It was a tiny minority that dropped out for good. Rather more dropped out for a year or two and then, the availability of jobs being what it was, dropped back in again. The majority were 'weekend hippies' just as their older brothers and sisters had been 'weekend ravers'. They rejected society in between getting on with their jobs or their education, but students in particular solved the philo-sophical difficulty that arose by resenting the minimal discipline that education imposed, and by regarding the degrees they were working more or less steadily towards as essentially worthless.

It was a teacher training college that I went to, but nobody I knew there had any intention of teaching at all.

▼ The Maharishi was hailed by the Beatles as offering an alternative to drugs. The guru told them their manager's death was 'not important'.

hello, i love you

The view was, in any case, widely held that nobody over thirty had anything valuable to say to anybody under thirty (an exception was made for gurus). On the contrary, the oldsters would do well to sit down and pay attention to what the youngsters had to say to *them*.

There was an international youth movement and there was a tremendous feeling that young people were suddenly important and they could change things. We were special and we had something to say and we were going to say it and they were going to listen!

The faith in more and better education (which had led the Robbins Committee in 1963 to propose the establishment of six new universities by the end of the decade) was now beginning to appear, to some observers, misplaced. Malcolm Muggeridge expressed his own doubts in a speech at Edinburgh University:

Education, it seems to me, has become a sort of mumbo-jumbo or cure-all for the ills of a Godless and decomposing society. Be it juvenile delinquency, high-school pregnancy or drug addiction among Brownies, the solution offered, whether by derelict politicians, high-minded life peeresses or humble radio panellists, is always the same: more education.

If one ventures to point out that places like, for instance, California – where more is spent on education, per head of population, than anywhere else in the world – are also famous in literature and in life for crimes of violence, moral depravity of every kind and a rate of lunacy high even by twentieth century standards, one only lays oneself open to a charge of obscurantism, if not downright fascism.

In 1968, when a wave of student unrest, taking the form of marches, sit-ins and strikes, hit several colleges and universities, it began to seem that they were indeed an ungrateful lot. But then, as one student argued on the radio:

We're supposed, apparently, to spend three or four years being pathetically grateful to a benevolent state for providing us with £360 a year, which just, if you don't drink or smoke, manages to keep body and soul together. I personally see no earthly reason why I should be particularly grateful to the state, to the rest of the nation, for giving me this. They're giving it to me for their own purposes, in order that I may do the things that I'm doing.

The student demos in the UK were almost entirely imitative of much more significant events overseas. They were inspired by the campus riots in America against the Vietnam war, and by 'Les Événements' of May '68 in Paris, where a joyously anarchistic student revolt was brutally put down by the French riot police, the CRS.

In our college, which was in South London, there was all this stuff about secret files on students, and the whole college walked out one day and sort of sat around on the grass and said, you know, 'Unless you don't keep files, unless you open the files up to us, we won't go to lectures.' And that was everybody, it wasn't just a few, it was everybody did that.

In America and in Paris, that was a completely different ball-game. We were just playing at it, we were just following the fashion, but it did have its roots in a very serious movement.

I didn't really like demonstrations because I felt that people were there for the sake of the chanting, for the sake of the marching, and it could have been about anything. They would have chanted and marched no matter what. Sorry if that sounds cynical, but that's how I actually felt at the time.

The Paris thing was very inspiring. It was the slogans like 'What do we want? Everything! When do we want it? Now!' … 'Imagination has seized power' … But it seemed that the impossible was actually just around the corner, that you really could break all the power structures and all the taboos and say 'This is what we want; this is what will happen. There will be no more greed, war, persecution, intolerance. All the evils of mankind will be eradicated.'

TOM EWELL
JAYNE MANSFIELD
EDMOND O'BRIEN.

20th CENTURY-FOX'S

THE GIRL CAN'T HELP IT!

COLOR by DE LUXE
CINEMASCOPE

AND INTRODUCING THE FOLLOWING
ROCK 'N' ROLL STARS
FATS DOMINO · THE PLATTERS
LITTLE RICHARD & HIS BAND
GENE VINCENT & HIS BLUE CAPS
THE TRENIERS · EDDIE FONTAINE
THE CHUCKLES · ABBEY LINCOLN
JOHNNY GLENN · NINO TEMPO
EDDIE COCHRAN

◄ Once Little Richard had starred in the same movie as Jayne Mansfield's thorax, the link between sex and rock 'n' roll became explicit.

▲ Blue Jean Baby ... Denim jeans were one of the first specifically teenage fashion trends of the fifties; an alternative, for girls, to the bell tent look.

◄ Britain's first rock 'n' roll star, Tommy Steele, inventor of the cliché about wanting to become an all-round entertainer.

By the mid-sixties, ▶
Elvis was earning a
million dollars and a
gold record for every
movie. Who needed
rock 'n' roll?

▲ The Who's first
album in 1965 was
one of the most
impressive debut LPs
ever. The union jacket
was considered
outrageously
satirical at the time.

Twiggy (Lesley ▶
Hornby), the face of
the late sixties, a
sensation at fifteen,
with her Svengali
boyfriend, Justin de
Villeneuve (Nigel
Davies).

◄Psychedelia was a
hiccup in the Stones'
career, marked by the
somewhat
embarrassing 'Their
Satanic Majesties
Request' LP.

▲During the sixties,
teenage bedroom
decor changed from
floral wallpaper to
sellotaped centre-
spread.

◄'Help' (1965). Not
so much a movie,
more a glossy
travelogue cum pop
promo, it helped to
turn the Beatles into
swinging sixties,
colour supplement
fantasy figures.

The guardsman ▶
look swept Carnaby
Street in 1966. A
colourful foretaste of
psychedelia, it was
part of a craze for
Victorian kitsch (as
in 'I was Lord
Kitchener's Valet', a
leading boutique of
the day).

▼ The round-collared
Beatle jacket was
originally designed by
Pierre Cardin. By the
time it was available
through mail order,
however, the Fab
Four had gone back to
lapels.

The owners of ▶
these gleaming
fetish-objects
wouldn't be far away:
with that much
nickable gear on their
machines, they
couldn't afford to be.

◄Jimi Hendrix, a walking acid trip. Guitarists are still trying to work out how he achieved some of those incredible noises.

▲Psychedelic posters and album sleeves often had religious overtones, borrowed from Islamic or Hindu devotional art or even stained glass windows.

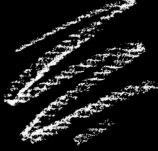

◄Woodstock, August 1969. Half a million peaceful people let it all hang out.

Dennis Hopper ▶
starred with Peter
Fonda in 'Easy Rider',
the key movie of the
late-hippie period. It
tells of two free-
spirited dope freaks
who get shot for
having long hair.

▼The Hell's Angels
showed up at all the
festivals in the early
seventies. It was
their self-appointed
role to keep the
citizens in line by
walking around
looking menacing.

The most important rock figure of the seventies, David Bowie created a series of stage personae, from Ziggy Stardust to the Thin White Duke, and – like Dylan – he knew when to move on.

Gary Glitter made ▶
Elvis in Vegas look
slim and understated.
The kids loved him
because they knew
that he knew that
they thought he was
hilarious.

◀Slade evolved from
a semi-skinhead,
soccer-and-stomp
band into pantomime
funsters, an antidote
to the seventies
disease of taking
rock music too
seriously.

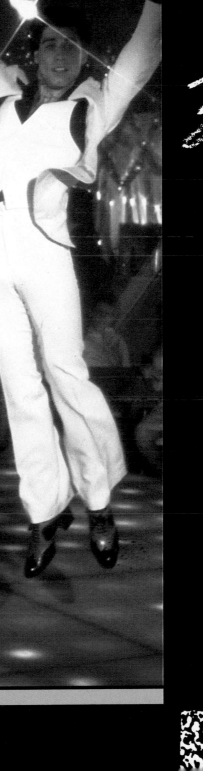

◄It was so easy to parody the John Travolta disco strut that anyone who attempted it was liable to be laughed at. Disco itself, however, kept on keeping on.

An executioner's ▶
mask and a
dismembered doll –
do-it-yourself
fashion accessories
which never quite
replaced the
matching shoes and
handbag.

▼Sue Catwoman and
punk pals take a
stroll. In the
beginning they
turned heads but, for
all except the
tourists, the shock
soon wore off.

◄By the early
eighties, the problem
of what to wear down
the disco was well-
nigh insuperable.
There were few hard-
and-fast rules, and
even fewer clues.

▼The 'northern soul'
discos had a late-
mod flavour and
featured a lot of
athletic showing-off
by the lads.

The 'oi' movement ▶
of the late seventies
combined elements
of both skinhead and
punk. The union jack
was now worn not as
a satirical comment
but as a statement of
right-wing beliefs.

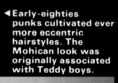

◄Early-eighties punks cultivated ever more eccentric hairstyles. The Mohican look was originally associated with Teddy boys.

New Romantics. ► The look flourished in the élite clubs but, perhaps understandably, was not much seen on the streets.

◄ Early-eighties teenage fashion, for the most part, avoided extremes. Pink eyeshadow and a pair of 'Bet Lynch' earrings were often as wild as a girl cared to get.

Punk as a parody of ▶ pornography. Escapees from the 'Rocky Horror Show' merge comfortably into the crowd at the Hippodrome.

Mod revivalists ▶
Paul Weller and Mick
Talbot of Style
Council. The
squeaky-clean image
lives on into the
eighties.

◀Gender-bender Boy
George in his prime,
'sowing seeds of
tolerance'.

▲ Duran Duran,
originally a New
Romantic group
remarkable for the
fact that all five were
pin-up pretty, starred
in some of the most
expensive videos of
the eighties.

Some looked even further afield for their inspiration. In 1967, John 'Hoppy' Hopkins, a leading figure in the underground, spoke on the radio of its aim to abolish money:

> It's no coincidence that the Red Guards made a pile of money sixty feet high in Peking and set fire to it. It was their own money. That's the connection between things that go on all over the world.

He did admit that it was not going to happen in London immediately.

Such theatrical public gestures, deeply significant or utterly meaningless according to 'where your head was at', were the essence of the late-sixties demo. When the students of Keele University surrounded the Vice-Chancellor's house at midnight and started humming, with the declared intention of levitating it 250 feet in the air, they carried such conviction that the radio reporter on the spot was heard to say, 'I must confess that I can't see, at the moment, any sign of movement...'

The big anti-Vietnam war demonstration in Grosvenor Square, for which these campus skirmishes had been small-scale rehearsals, was similarly infused with the feeling that everybody present was playing a part, this time in some epic remake of *Doctor Zhivago*, in which the Tom Courtenay role would be played by Tariq Ali. Chanting and jeering, flags and banners, cavalry charges, ball bearings under the horses' hoofs, blood streaming down faces, smoke bombs and fireworks, flour bombs and red paint, it had everything except the bayonets.

It was the theatre of demonstration. I was throwing stones and clods of earth at the American Embassy and being mown down by guys on horseback, certainly, but it was never intended to be violent. Of course that was the interesting dilemma, that we had to demonstrate against a violent war, but peacefully. So we were sitting down in the street, singing songs, holding flowers. But I don't think the Establishment liked it very much so they provoked us into a little bit more of an extreme reaction than we would have liked ourselves. We thought we were quite rational in our protest against the war, and I think what's interesting about youth is that you really

▼ **March 1968: 15,000 demonstrators fight to reach the American Embassy in Grosvenor Square, while cameramen, for whose benefit the battle was staged, dutifully recorded the mayhem.**

hello,
i love you

believe that if you present a very reasoned argument to people in authority then they will listen and perhaps adapt their policy.

Speaking on behalf of the Government, Mr James Callaghan observed that Mr Tariq Ali was a spoiled, rich playboy whom the media of mass communication had elevated to a distinction that a squalid nuisance did not really command. The bombing of Vietnam continued.

The toughest test of hippie idealism was what they were to do about money. The state was fair game, of course, but grants and dole money, useful as they were, would not stretch to the purchase of very many Jefferson Airplane records, so they fell back on the economic system which Mark Twain had described as 'taking in one another's washing'. They made and sold each other clothes, patchouli-scented candles, hubble-bubble pipes, posters and rhubarb wine. They wholesaled Greek shoulder-bags, joss sticks, drugs and underground newspapers. They organised rent parties, whip-rounds for petrol and bring-your-own-carrot soup-making sessions.

This was known as the alternative economy and, as is the way with economies, it made some people richer and others poorer. Most schemes of communal living began in a glow of mutual generosity and ended in everyone writing their names on their eggs in the fridge. The 'white bicycle' scheme was tried in Oxford: the idea, borrowed from the anarchists of Amsterdam, was that bikes would be painted white and left unlocked, so that anyone could use whatever bike was nearest to hand when they needed one. The scheme lasted about a week before the city was full of securely-locked bicycles freshly-painted in every imaginable colour except white.

You took what you wanted and you gave something back in return, and it was very much a give-and-take kind of idea. When we bought the house together, there were five of us and I think the idea was that we had a commitment to living together. We did believe that if you lived with your friends and if you had children, then they were brought up together with the other people who were equally responsible, so we bought the house together, we did up

the house together, and it worked for a while.

We ate together, so when we sat down for a meal there were about fourteen people who had different ideas, who were involved politically or who were involved, say, in certain crafts, actually creative people, and I think it really worked. I think we did care about each other. I think there was an awful lot of mutual support. You knew that if you were ill or in trouble there would be at least five or six people around you who would help you, who would look after you. And that's really important. A lot of people don't have that at all. People don't have it from their own families.

There was a kind of folk culture that we were all into at the time. You know, eating brown rice and making your own patchwork and listening to the Incredible String Band. It was all 'back to the earth', 'Mother Earth', and whether it was phoney or not was difficult for a lot of people to distinguish.

No hippie could credibly live at home with Mum and Dad, so there had to be a 'pad'. For those who could manage rent, or a lump-sum contribution towards the purchase of a run-down inner-city terraced house or a country cottage, all was well. For others, the answer was to squat. Squatting – moving into an empty property and living there until the lengthy and complicated mechanism of eviction had run its course – had two advantages: it was a revolutionary gesture, and it made for cheap accommodation. The best-publicised squat took place in September 1969 at a 100-room mansion in Piccadilly, overlooking Hyde Park corner. It was organised by the London Street Commune, whose spokesman was interviewed on the radio:

–I take it you don't have enough money to buy a hotel room, is that it?
–Yes, that's right.
–Is that because you don't have a job?
–Yes.
–Well, aren't there plenty of jobs going? Can't you go out and get one?

◄ The squat at 144, Piccadilly. Access was achieved via a ladder, an improvised drawbridge and a window.

–There are plenty of jobs going, but I'm a poet and I can't get a job as a poet.

By the end of the decade, the hippies had moved out of San Francisco and were living in the hills. Similarly in the UK there was a move away from the inner cities and into the countryside. Donovan, the hippiest hippie ever to make a million, bought his own island off the coast of Scotland. He later explained:

I got this island because there was going to be a terrific atomic war, you see. I was going to go out and grow some vegetables and live on my own or with my close communal friends, and we were going to build an alternative, tiny little society up there, and when the bomb came we'd all survive and we'd build the world again from there.

The record producer Micky Most described what happened:

It all sounds great when you think about it, but when you've got to do it, you know, you've got to get elec-

tricity there, you've got to get running water and sanitation and all that, plus you've got to have these people that you need and they have to be professional farmers, and of course they weren't, they were real layabouts. And the place, instead of becoming a beautiful island, looked like one of those concentration camps in the end.

'Equisexual', the *International Times* had promised at the beginning, and that too was an ideal that disappeared down a hole somewhere between theory and practice.

I mean that Earth Mother bit was such a con, the biggest con ever, I think. I mean it was just really looking after the kids, doing all the washing, being in fact the ideal mother but with this sex bit thrown in too. I don't know how people fell for it, I really don't. I don't think I did. Well I hope I didn't.

Quite recently I saw some old copies of 'Oz' and I was just amazed at how much they hated women. I mean women are just breasts and . . . whatever. Because all those magazines, although they went through the obscenity trial and the rest of

hello, i love you

it and people said they were very free, actually they're about men screwing women. That's what it's about, basically.

Jim Haynes (whose autobiography is entitled *Thanks for Coming!* and is dedicated to some 2000 people whose names fill nineteen pages) wrote to *Oz* as follows:

How is this for a beautiful, mad idea? Would it not be fun if, in every part of the world, a bell could be sounded every day at a different time, and when you heard the bell, you stopped cooking, eating, walking, talking, etc., and made love with the person (or persons) nearest you, no matter what their age or sex!

The impact of such beautiful, mad notions on the population at large can be judged by the fact that a survey in 1970 of teenagers' opinions on sex found 64% opposed to intercourse outside marriage, while most of the remainder were in favour of 'trial marriage' but not of casual affairs.

What was different about the hippie generation was that the minority who did distribute their sexual favours more widely than that, like the minority who regularly used drugs, steadfastly refused to feel guilty about it.

The very important thing that changed was that it filtered down that it was actually all right to say yes, that you weren't an absolute outcast if you weren't a virgin. Before that, if you weren't a virgin you were sort of second class and nobody would want to go out with you. But it became possible that you could say yes, and you could tell people, and you didn't have to hide it, and you could be quite proud. And it got to the point where you could boast about the number of lovers you had had rather than keeping it a terrible, terrible secret. That's what changed.

It doesn't need to be said. The Pill and the 1967 Abortion Act made all the difference. I just didn't have to think about whether I would sleep with a boyfriend or not. I knew that I could do whatever I liked.

There was so much more choice. You didn't have to get married and have children, you didn't have to become pregnant: so I think that was a real liberation for women.

What could be said about this in public was still somewhat limited. The Rolling Stones appeared on the American 'Ed Sullivan Show' to perform their record 'Let's Spend The Night Together', and delivered instead a mumbled 'Let's Spend Some Time Together'. Mick Jagger stoutly insisted that the lyric did not in any case imply any sexual impropriety.

In the early days of Radio One, John Peel was chastised by his employers for mentioning to listeners that he had once had VD. Five years before it would have seemed incredible that he should have done such a thing; now it seemed incredible that the BBC should mind.

Everybody took their clothes off at festivals. At Woodstock and even at the Isle of Wight a lot of people took their clothes off. And it was all all right!

The names of two pop festivals, Woodstock and Altamont, are used as short-

▼ Festivals brought the hippie tribe together. Some saw them as the beginnings of an alternative society, others as a chance to get stoned and/or laid.

hand to represent the zenith and nadir respectively of the hippie ideal. Woodstock, 'three days of peace, music and love' as they said on the poster of the film of the festival, brought together half a million people on a farm in upstate New York in August 1969. There, in a haze of pot-smoke, sustained by sandwiches donated as an emergency measure by the Women's Group of the local Jewish Community Centre, and doing their best to forget that the portable toilets were overflowing, they danced and hollered in the most peaceable manner possible.

Altamont, a free concert by the Rolling Stones at a speedway outside San Francisco, should have been like that, or at least like the concert they'd given in Hyde Park that summer. But this one, in the last month of the sixties, went horribly wrong. The Hell's Angels, hired to keep the crowd in order, behaved like the stormtroopers whose swastikas they wore. Marty Balin of Jefferson Airplane was knocked unconscious, Mick Jagger was punched in the face and a man named Meredith Hunter was stabbed to death in front of the stage.

Nothing in Britain matched the scale of Woodstock (let alone the violence of Altamont), but the nearest thing to it was the Isle of Wight Festival in August 1969.

Thousands of people were there, thousands and thousands, and we had a tent but lots of people came with just dustbin bags and were sleeping on the ground.

There was some sense of community in the fact that there were a hundred thousand people there, all reasonably peaceful, and it wasn't just because they were stoned out of their minds.

The whole experience was extremely impressive. Everybody was extremely nice to everybody else. It was a tremendous feeling of happiness and love. You could leave your bag on the ground, walk away, and it would be there when you got back. And people were very kind to one another. People were giving things away to each other.

Twelve months later they did it all again. Once more 100,000 gathered on the Isle of Wight, but somehow it wasn't the same. The difference had to do with a certain loss of innocence. The *Daily Telegraph* reported that the police were looking for a 'pusher' who had been going among the crowd selling curry powder as marijuana. A true hippie would not have been cynical enough to perpetrate such a trick, or naive enough to fall for it.

('The kids at the Isle of Wight were being totally controlled and manipulated by superpigs', said Jean-Jacques Lebel, who led the move to smash down the fences around the festival site. 'They had to pay exorbitantly for their own music and they became completely exhausted, sleeping in the lavatories, hungry, so weary they were pissing over each other . . .')

The general feeling that the end of the decade marked the end of an era was intensified by the deaths within two years of Brian Jones, Jimi Hendrix, Janis Joplin and Jim Morrison. Each had been identified with the sex'n'drugs'n'rock'n'roll culture; each was, in a profound sense, a martyr to it.

Hendrix was a black Heathcliff, a wild maniacal figure, a wizard of the guitar on the stage. I mean he made love to it, set it on fire, and you know, it was violent and it was sensual as well.

When he was on stage, pouring lighter fluid over the guitar, setting fire to it and then whirling it round and round his head so you could hear the flames humming through the strings with the amps turned full up, and then demolishing the speaker stack and you could hear it all going CRUNCH, CRUNCH. . . . Is it music or is it lifestyle? Or is it what we need in the modern world, the multi-media performance, the whole-life performance, and you have to die to stay with it?

Yes, he 'lived the life' in that he took a lot of acid. Well that was his life, really, wasn't it? LSD plus rock. And that, perhaps, for a lot of people was what life was about.

Hendrix, Joplin, Jones, all those people . . . It's not just their music, it's their encapsulation of the life-style that their world wanted to follow. There they are, living a surrogate life for all the people in

hello, i love you

the audience, who go some of the way but don't have anything like the resources or the sheer nerve to go as far as they did. 'Life in the fast lane', that was the choice of the sixties, and they epitomised that life-style, and dying of it was really the only way out.

What was left of hippiedom appeared to go haywire: Charles Manson, a stereotype hippie if ever there was one, committed foul murder under the influence (he claimed) of a Beatles LP; the far-left had moved on from burning the Stars and Stripes in Grosvenor Square to applauding the deaths of British soldiers in Belfast; Jim Haynes, Germaine Greer and other pillars of the anti-establishment were running a 'European Sex-paper' called *Suck*, which in December 1970 announced plans for the Wet Dream Festival, a four-day pornographic film-show in Amsterdam with such added attractions as a masturbation contest and a bondage-wear fashion show. That month, Richard Neville wrote in *Oz* that some of his best friends were going straight, cutting their hair, wearing suits and seeking respectable jobs. He was discouraged, he said, by escalating instances of brutality among 'heads' and by the 'social style' which had become pretentious and uncommunicative. As an example of what he meant, Neville quoted the case of Victor Herbert, a sponsor of the *International Times*, the Living Theatre and other underground institutions:

▼ *Oz* editor Richard Neville and his girl-friend Louise. The magazine's conviction for obscenity brought martyrdom to Neville and his co-defendants. While on remand they were given prison hair-cuts.

Victor contributes to the movement what he calls 'space', i.e. his enormous residence as a crashpad. Current guests include a poet who came for a weekend two years ago and won't budge, a pair of video heads, remnants of the Living Theatre and several nameless others. The atmosphere created by most of these super-hip freeloaders manages to be simultaneously hostile, slovenly and as exclusive as White's club. Membership to the inner sanctum revolves around facility with drugs and as the pleasant Victor himself is rather slow on the draw he is excluded, in spirit, from his own house.

'We blithely declare World War III on our parents,' Neville concluded, 'and yet have already forgotten how to smile at our friends.'

The greater the illusion has been, the more bitter is the disillusionment when it ends. For the weekend hippies it wasn't so bad; they had been in the real world all along, and it had done them no harm to taste a little freedom, a little hope, a little peace and love, and it left its mark.

People were getting much more tolerant of each other and much more compassionate and understanding. You know, they were beginning to be tolerant of gays, whereas in the fifties they'd been beaten up and put in prison. There was all that kind of social stuff going on. You just took it for granted really. It's only now when you look back that you realise there was great progress made.

The guru of the American acid generation, Leary, when he was asked what had happened to all the flowers, he said 'Well, they went to seed, just like flowers do.' And there's a lot of truth in that. I mean, we've got a sixties king coming up in Prince Charles. He can't escape this shadow of the sixties. He's read his Jungian psychology, you know. He knows about thinking like that. He knows about alternative medicine. He's interested in small-scale operations. You know, he can't escape his inheritance.

skinhead moonstomp

'It was a military uniform: you had your jeans, your braces, your steel-capped boots on. I mean, the Army wear boots, don't they? As a military unit you wear boots. They was a weapon. If someone was having a go at you, you could put the boot in.'

skinhead moonstomp

Skinheads? Well, there's always a status quo of prats around — they just go under different names really.

Among the long-haired thousands who gathered in Grosvenor Square at the end of October 1968 to chant 'Victory to the NLF!' and 'Ho, Ho, Ho Chi Minh!', there were 200 shaven-headed supporters of Millwall Football Club who were chanting 'Enoch, Enoch!' and 'Students, students, ha, ha, ha!' Nobody yet called them skinheads, but they had not gone unnoticed; only the previous month the new style had achieved mention in the *Daily Telegraph*:

▼ **Traditional Bank Holiday seaside skirmishing in the late sixties showed mods changing gradually into boots-and-braces skinheads.**

Hundreds of youths in hobnailed boots left Margate last night after a weekend of fights and scuffles with police. The boot brigade, successors to the mods and rockers, met police in several clashes on the seafront yesterday and on Sunday. One boy, sixteen, dressed in hill-billy fashion in heavy brown boots, and jeans held up by braces, said: 'The boots are just part of the uniform. They make us look hard.'

Skinhead style was not so much an innovation as a standardisation of the 'hard mod' image, which could trace its ancestry all the way back to Clacton 1964, but while undeniably neat, the look was about as unstylish as it was possible to get: shaved head, big boots (Doc Martens, also known as 'cherry reds'), wide jeans rolled up to mid-calf and worn with braces which went *over* the sleeveless pullover that was worn as a vest, and, for very cold weather, the Harrington jacket, a short, black denim 'bomber' jacket with a checked lining. For evening wear, to go 'clubbing it', the skinhead dressed more formally in two-tone Tonik trousers, a Ben Sherman button-down shirt and Brut aftershave.

We'd just gone through the mod era, which we'd all appreciated. I mean, we sat round with our scooters in the early days. We all went down to Brighton and Southend, Bank Holidays, and we all had a fight with the greasers like the mods did. But then we went to the extreme: I mean, we took our hair right down to the limit, you know, half an inch or whatever. I had it done at a barbers' called Grey's down East India Dock Road. It wasn't much of a haircut; he just gets those old trimmers out and goes zing, zing, zing and that's it, your hair's gone!

By this time, the notion that no youth cult was complete without its own philosophy had taken such a hold on the nation in general and the Press in particular that reporters were put out to discover that skinheads didn't seem to believe in anything very much. The *Daily Mail* quoted a sixteen-year-old 'peanut' as saying: 'What are we for? Nothing really. We are just a group of blokes. We're not *for* anything.' Asked what he was *against*, however, the peanut waxed verbose: 'Long hair, pop, hippie sit-ins, live-ins and the long-haired cult of non-violence.' The term 'peanut', the *Mail* added helpfully, was 'a sneering description of the cult, directed more at their rattling motor-scooters ("peanuts in a tin") than at their shaven heads'. (This analysis of the minutiae of youth culture was typical of the period. No gang of skinheads was complete without its own non-judgemental sociologist in tow.)

By the summer of 1969, the young nihilists were proving a serious nuisance to the alternative society. In June, *Oz* reported:

The Spikeys, or Brushcuts, are summer's new dumb terrorists in jeans, braces and thick leather boots. With sharpened aluminium combs and hair to match (*sic*) they have already wrecked one major free concert. They maraud in large groups, and last month beat up a few long-hairs in Hyde Park, to the baying accompaniment of vastly outnumbering hippies: 'Wow, what a bad scene, man.' One compensation: only the masculine variety have been spotted, so at least they won't breed.

(*Oz* spoke too soon).

The *Black Dwarf*, in August, fed the whole puzzle into the sausage-machine of Marxist dialectical analysis and cranked out the theory that skinheads . . .

represent an assertion of working-class identity against the hippies and lefties – groups that they very reasonably consider middle-class and irrelevant to their life-situation ... The skinheads are the real drop-outs, as opposed to the fancy drop-outs who take a few months off work to do very nicely living by their wits. These latter people aren't really drop-outs at all, they are people whose dissatisfaction with society had led them to take a long holiday from it. The skinhead is rejected *by* society. He is *dropped* out – because he is thick, because he can't cope with responsibility, because he's disorganised. He lands up in the lowest-paid job where he has to work long, boring, unrewarding, unrecognised hours before

skinhead moonstomp

◄ **Skinheads didn't worry too much about fashion details. Criticism was unlikely to be expressed.**

skinhead moonstomp

going back to a home that has blatantly missed out on the glitter of the affluent society.

What was to be done about it? *Black Dwarf* proposed to 'mobilise' the 'many thousands of working-class boys and girls in this country who were deeply impressed by the May Events in France, for whom the word "revolution" is an exciting word.... These young people ... see the skinheads as the nasty, thick little louts they really are.'

The class-based explanation understates one important point about skinheads: they were reacting not only against the upwardly-mobile grammar-grubs, but also against what they saw as the effeminacy of the hippie image. Their own style was a parody of butchness, and they saw 'queer-bashing', by which they meant taunting and assaulting the frillier varieties of male hippie, as a moral crusade.

They were mostly from the secondary modern schools and they mostly left school as fifteen and went either on the dole or stacking shelves in supermarkets, that sort of thing. They weren't what you call the cream of the intelligentsia.

Against the lumpen-prole stereotype one should set the 1968 report on soccer hooliganism which analysed 497 convictions; it found that 10% of the offenders were skilled workers, a further 4% clerks and salesmen, and there were even a couple of managerial-grade yobbos in the sample. Less than half were unskilled or unemployed.

I went to college. I'm an electrician by trade, and touch wood I've never been unemployed. You know, several others who were in our gang are in business now. One of them is an architect surveyor with a half-million-pound turnover and two villas in Spain. He got done for having a row at Coventry, I remember. He got three months' D.C. (Detention Centre) for steaming into the Old Bill with a hammer.

All these things what we was to the older people – hooligans, louts, tearaways – you know, it's not true. I mean I like to think I'm a likeable person as such. Maybe I wasn't so much then, but even then I was polite and never disrespectful to elderly

people. I had neighbours who'd say 'Oh, he's a lovely boy, helped me home with my shopping yesterday' and all that. I mean, just because I done things on a Saturday afternoon on the terraces and Friday night at the club, it doesn't make me a bad person.

Insofar as skinheads *were* recruited from among society's rejects (and as always, to articulate the thought was half-way to making it true), their constituency was on the increase as the swinging sixties gave way to the sour seventies. In August 1971, *The People*, under a headline that was not yet a cliché, 'FROM SCHOOL TO THE SCRAP-HEAP', expressed its concern:

It's going to take longer than ever this year for school-leavers to find their first jobs. Obviously and tragically. For a record 450,000 boys and girls left school last month to join the record queue of more than 800,000 unemployed. And, until Britain's sagging economy revives, job-hunting teenagers are in for the worst period of blighted prospects since the war.

Meanwhile, the *Evening Standard* blamed not unemployment but the schools:

When they leave school they will still be so illiterate they will get lost on the Underground. Already they know that they are failures and they resent it. Knowing no other language, at twelve or thirteen they adopt the ways of the misfit: get convict haircuts and act violently. Their number grows each year, their behaviour becomes more extreme. They represent, without doubt, one of the major challenges to our education system. Education Minister Mrs Margaret Thatcher described as 'the most shattering set of statistics I have ever had to give' the following: that 91% of children who leave school at fifteen (and nearly half the population still does leave at fifteen) had no exam passes of any kind.

If evidence is needed that skinheads, in the beginning, were not consciously

racist, one need only point to their favourite music.

Music-wise it was reggae. Well, I call it reggae, I mean it was kind of bluebeat. It was Prince Buster and Desmond Dekker and the Upsetters and the Pioneers to name but a few. The first record I can remember buying – which everyone went mad over – was 'Red Red Wine' by Tony Tribe. That was the first single I bought.

To go with the Jamaican ska music, with its heavy off-beat, the skinheads evolved their own semi-military style of dancing, the skinhead stomp.

You'd go three steps one way and three steps the other and two forward and one back and kick your leg behind you. Everyone seemed to dance the same way. It wouldn't take you two minutes to pull a bird, you know. The birds would all be going like that up and down the floor and you'd just stand in front of them and just follow them and that's it   you'd clocked it with a bird, you know.

The *Sunday Times*, in September 1969, even theorised that the skinhead hair-cut as well as the music was borrowed from 'Negroes, whom they call Calebs or "Rudies" and whom they leave pretty much alone'.

This happy state of racial harmony was undermined and finally destroyed by the emergence in 1969 and the spread in 1970 of the ugly sport of 'Paki-bashing'. It started in the East End, reflecting the hostility of the wider working class community to a large-scale influx of Asian immigrants at the time. One suspects, also, that skinheads picked on Asians, in the same way as they picked on hippies, 'queers' and students, because they were less likely than West Indians to attempt to defend themselves. 'Pakis', because of wider cultural differences from working-class whites, were despised. West Indians – although they might be fought against, much as Tottenham supporters would fight Arsenal fans – were regarded with respect, or at least with as much respect as one can actually feel while kicking somebody in the face.

Yes, we did have trouble with the blacks. I mean, there was a club that started up at Mile End that was called 'The A Train' and yeah, sure, every Friday night, every Saturday night, whenever we chose to go up there, we'd have a battle with the blacks. But we had black guys on our side as well, a few coloured guys who'd stand behind you and fight for you as a brother, no problem.

A black Liverpudlian remembers the fights in his city as having more to do with territory than with race. They certainly were not all one-sided.

Oh yeah, we used to fight against the skinheads, and it'd be like territorial. You'd have to stay within your territory. Like you wouldn't get one man coming out of his territory, going into say Lodge Lane, because you'd just get attacked. So we used to meet them at certain times, and we'd throw bricks and people would have

skinhead moonstomp

▼ Desmond Dekker sang jaunty ska songs that were good to stomp along to. He even had the right hair-cut.

skinhead moonstomp

catapults, you know? And of a Saturday, people would go into town, the city centre, and they'd go in the precinct there, in a café called the Brass Rail. The black guys would meet in there and the skinheads would come in shouting all kinds of things, 'Niggers' and 'Wogs', and then you'd get the kind of situation where you'd have ten black guys and say fifty skinheads, and if the ten black guys made a dash for the skinheads, the fifty of them would run, you know, because they'd see plenty of black faces and they'd see ten as like fifty of them.

And then people started getting into karate and ju-jitsu. There were the Bruce Lee films and they appealed to the black guys and they started learning kung fu. Then after a while, the Bruce Lee thing died out and people started to leave it, and there wasn't this need to fight the skinheads. As people grew up they got more mature and got more sense, and that type of thing stopped.

The danger that the latent racism of the skinheads could be worked upon to the point where it became the cult's *raison d'être* had been spotted by *Black Dwarf*, which headlined its 1969 article 'THE SKINHEADS – A YOUTH GROUP FOR THE NATIONAL FRONT?' It was a while, however, before the NF made significant progress in that direction. Skinheads had more important things to do than attend meetings and listen to speeches. They were fellow-travellers of the far right but they were seldom card-carrying members.

It surprised some people, but the attempt to create a latter-day brownshirt movement was a failure, and the Front began to concentrate on reincarnating the *Hitlerjugend* instead. They began to spread their propaganda in schools, forming their own student association for the purpose. Matters were to come to a head later in the decade, but for most early-seventies skinheads, 'ideology' was altogether too long a word.

From their mod forebears, skinheads inherited their drug of choice, amphetamine, which had a lot to do with their edgy, aggressive stance; a skinhead on speed was a thick ear waiting to happen.

You'd stand there, you had your chewing-gum, you'd be chewing away and talking to your mates and you'd say 'Who's he looking at?' and you'd pump yourself up and you'd start getting paranoid about 'Is he looking at me? Is he looking at me?' and the guy, who was probably innocently watching a bird or whatever, when you'd say 'Who you looking at?' he'd say the wrong answer and you'd just biff him, you know what I mean? And then it would all go off. He'd have a couple of mates and it'd all go off. And once it all goes and the glasses are smashing and you hear them smashing you just run in there. There's no thought about the glass coming in your face or the punch in the earhole or somebody jabbing you in the back with a knife . . .

Skinheads were frightening in groups, but on their own they were a bit pathetic really, because they needed to be in a pack. But you never knew at the time whether any of them were carrying knives or not. I used to carry a blooming great Norton chain just for self-protection. But you used to wonder how these things ever got used in the first place. Obviously someone draws a weapon first and you wonder if it's worth while . . .

People came at us with chains and lumps of wood and lumps of metal. And you either stand your ground or you back off a bit and see if you can pick up a bit of debris or something and steam back and see whose bottle goes then. And I mean you can get hurt. I've seen people get stabbed, I've seen glasses put in people's faces, I've seen terrible things. Touch wood I haven't had it happen to me. I'm not saying I wasn't involved in doing it the other way round.

No mod would have been seen dead in a football stadium, but the terraces became the skinheads' public stage and their recruiting ground. They followed soccer in the first place because it was part of a working-class tradition and they were class conservatives. It also offered them a community with which to identify, a territory to defend and the opportunity, without the inconvenience of having to make arrangements as to time and place, to hit people.

Soccer's steady decline in importance as a spectator sport had been

briefly arrested in the late sixties; England had won the World Cup in 1966, and the lifting of restrictions on players' wages had made the professional footballer a much more glamorous figure, with the likes of George Best and Charlie George acquiring virtual pop star status.

At certain grounds – in Glasgow and Liverpool for example – it had long been the custom for the younger and more vocal supporters to mass at one end of the stadium and form a 'kop choir'. Now they developed more elaborate rituals, such as the massed, swaying rendition by Liverpool fans of the Mersey classic 'You'll Never Walk Alone'. The visiting supporters took these conventions back with them to their home grounds; the Arsenal 'North Bank', the first to become overtly skinhead, was established during the 1966–7 season and within a couple of years every major club acquired an 'end'. Within its tribal structure there were specialised roles, from the strategists and tacticians to the 'hard men' and 'nutters'. There was also the 'brains crew' who had the job of supplying witty remarks and appropriate songs at particular points in the game.

So far so jolly, but before the end could begin to sway and harmonise together it had first to be occupied. It became the aim of the visiting supporters to seize and hold the home fans' end, and thus, from the moment tho turnstiles were unlocked, did hostilities commence.

To say it was electrifying would be underestimating it. I mean you can talk about taking speed and smoking pot, but the actual buzz of being there and the noise generating round you and your team comes out and you scream ... It's like a really high buzz. Your hair stands up on end. It's like ... Did you see that film, 'Zulu'? The thin red line and these thousands of black men all steaming down on them? I should imagine that could make you feel something like it, that battle, that chant, you know, it's electrifying. Your hair stands up and you go all cold ... It's untrue.

... And all of a sudden, literally ten thousand Norwich supporters ran right across the pitch at Watford and the police just couldn't control us. They started

skinhead moonstomp

◄ **Publishers cashed in on the cults with a series of paperbacks on the theme of juvenile delinquency.** *Skinhead* **was followed by** *Skinhead Girls, Suedehead* **and even** *Glam.*

▼ **A late-seventies skin displays his literary influences. 'BM' stands for British Movement.**

skinhead moonstomp

throwing us back where they could, but we'd get in somewhere else, and the Watford supporters just made a mass exodus out of the ground and we just completely took over the other stand. Nowadays that would be regarded as hooliganism, but that never even made the papers.

We went to Coventry, I don't know how many of us, I suppose about 1500. We walked through the streets of Coventry. We went in Woolworths through one door, we came out the other door and they was still walking in Woolworths, it was like a big snake going through the chain store. And there was things picked up, aerosol paint sprays and all that. There was a couple of birds in front of us and we sprayed their legs blue and red, the colours of our team, and there was a man's motorbike — we sprayed that an entirely different colour. Anyway, we got to the match and for some reason they let us get in first, so we've got the centre of their stand, and we all started chanting. And then all of a sudden we could hear 'Cov-en-tree, Cove-en-tree . . .' It was like stereo, and they came steaming in from both sides and we was stuck in the middle. They slaughtered us!

Deviancy amplification did the rest: the supporters who didn't care for 'aggro' stayed at home, so the 'tiny hooligan minority' to whom club chairmen were so fond of referring became a rather larger minority and eventually (swelled by recruits for whom aggro was the main attraction) on some terraces became the majority.

The skinhead cult was the first post-war youth movement to which music was not of central importance. Football was, to them, what rock'n'roll had been to the Teddy boys. The soccer obsession was exploited by some pop performers such as Rod Stewart and Slade who achieved a sort of Cup Final atmosphere at their concerts, all swaying scarves and singalong choruses. But even out of season the skinhead's idea of a good time had little to do with concerts, discos or juke-boxes and far more to do with spending time in the pub or drinking on the move, endlessly discussing and occasionally committing acts of mindless violence.

We used to go out to the pub on a Friday night, then go clubbing it, then go out for a ride, generally just getting stoned, crash out somewhere in a forest or a lay-by somewhere, get up in the morning, drive back to London, have our breakfast, go home, get changed, meet again in the afternoon and be out drinking again then until Sunday night.

As with any extreme youth style, the skinheads attracted an outer fringe (or stubble) who went some but not all of the way. These tended to be younger and to include a higher proportion of girls. Someone coined the term 'suede-heads' for them, but they were more usually known as 'crombies' after their favourite coats. There were a few skin-head girls who attached themselves to the male gangs, where they were tolerated but largely ignored. Most girls who affected the style were at the pubescent stage of going round in little gangs of their own.

My first thing was a very half-hearted, ill-informed attempt to try and become a skinhead. I didn't know there was anything else to be. You wore a checked shirt and sort of broguey shoes, and there were also Crombie coats. I think they would have quite suited me, but it was not to be — I wore a Marks and Spencers school anorak.

In middle-class, suburban Merseyside we were all trying to be skinheads, which was really pathetic. We just weren't that hard, you know. And we used to go round in little Harrington jackets and boys' brogue shoes and have our hair cut really short except for those wisps at the side and the back. But I was very ill during that whole winter because I would insist on going round with this stupid jacket on.

The skinhead style was too simple and too well-rooted in ancient working-class traditions to do anything so final as dying out. It mutated, each mutation calling itself by a different name ('smooth-heads', 'casuals', 'oi') and re-emerged in a slightly different form (the post-punk 'skins') at the end of the seventies. Meanwhile the original skinheads were heading rapidly for middle age, the first teenage generation to mark the transition to adult respectability by growing their hair.

in a broken dream

'If you had very long hair, then you could wear anything. You know, you could wear an old man's mackintosh or a plastic mac or something and because you had long hair it looked vaguely sort of hip. But if you had short hair you just looked like a prat in a mackintosh.'

in a broken dream

The problem with the sixties show was nobody knew how to bring it to an end. It had come from nowhere and nobody knew how to bring the curtain down on it, so it just dribbled on and on and on, and the acts got more and more peculiar and the audience eventually knew that the show had left them, that it was no longer theirs, and it was finished long before it was finished.

Old flares never dye, they only fade away, and get more patches and more stains and become very ragged round the bottom. So it was with the hippies: the dregs of the movement lumbered on into the seventies, the undead, unable to be set to rest with a stake through the heart because there wasn't a heart any more. They say that, after death, the hair keeps on growing. The hippies continued to attract recruits because, if you didn't want to be bourgeois on the one hand or a shaven-headed moron on the other, there wasn't much else to be in 1971, but they knew they'd missed the magic bus.

I just regretted that I was born into the wrong age really. It felt like a bit of bad luck. Remembering the sixties, everything seemed to close up in the seventies and you

▼ Late-hippie style: loon pants, patches and 'ethnic' embroidery.

could almost visualise it being a darker period. I can sort of remember sunny days in the sixties, and in the seventies it didn't seem so apparent.

There is an internal mechanism which drives all cultural movements towards mannerism, the meaningless repetition of outer forms which gradually become more extreme without recapturing the lost essence of the classic period. In the case of the hippies it took the form of shabbier clothes, more and harder drugs, louder and more pretentious music.

You all wore battered, tattered clothes that you wouldn't nowadays give to a jumble sale, and the more battered and tattered you looked, the more of a hippie you were.

Anti-fashion ... it's actually not caring about what you wear. I mean of course you do. I mean if you're going to object to fashion through some conscious demonstration of dressing unfashionably, then that's actually caring enough not to care, if you see what I mean.

I used to look a real mess. I look back at photographs and I think 'Christ, if that was one of mine I wouldn't want to be seen out with it.'

My jeans were literally a sea of patches. I used to take great care in sewing new patches on, and it was also useful for hiding dope in ...

One of the outer forms to which the hippie dregs clung ever more assiduously was underground music, now itself fragmented into a hundred styles of 'progressive rock' and encompassing also the introspections of James Taylor, Carole King and others. This was music designed to be heard in one of two ways: either in a huge stadium over an earth-trembling P.A. system, or at home on a very expensive stereo hi-fi.

Records started to become a private thing; until then they had been a public thing, they were background music or they were for dancing. Now, in the early seventies, you listened to them in a darkened room and learned the finer points. It was loud and all-encompassing and there were no distractions. That was the intensity of it.

As soon as I got a record-player it sort of liberated me from my parents, and I ended up staying in my bedroom for most of the seventies, playing records, having friends up and the joss-sticks would go on and we stayed up till two in the morning and then crawled out for school next morning. That was the major form of entertainment really.

Record sales in Britain, which had declined in the mid-sixties from their 1964 peak, climbed steadily throughout the early seventies until they were double the figure for the Beatles' heyday, at 200,000,000 units sold. Moreover most of these were LPs, which in 1970 began to out-sell singles. In 1972 the American music industry outgrossed Hollywood. As the underground press declined, the circulations of the music papers such as *Melody Maker* and *New Musical Express* increased. In the first four years of the decade they went up by 50%. A significant number of rock stars became multi-millionaires, having grown wise in the ways of tax avoidance and profit maximisation (live abroad, write and publish your own songs, start your own record company). Mick Jagger had a villa in France, a house in Ireland, a flat in Chelsea and a mansion in Jamaica. Since it was now ludicrous for such people to hold the hippie pose, the period was marked by a gradual shedding, on the part of the rock heroes, of their hypocrisy about money.

In pop's innocent years, the teenagers bought records because they liked them. Then they bought the records because they liked the groups. Now they bought the records because they liked the musicians who played in the groups. Individual superstars, 'guitar heroes', formed and re-formed endless 'supergroups', their every split and coalescence breathlessly charted by the music press. Bands began to sound like firms of solicitors: Emerson, Lake and Palmer; Crosby, Stills, Nash and Young; Bruce West and Laing. The guitar hero became the most potent fantasy image of the time.

In fact my school report summed it up: 'Studies played a poor second to extra-curricular activities' it said on my final exam report, which didn't mean that I dropped out and failed miserably, it just meant that I dreamed a bit in school. I'd

gaze out of the window and see myself in a classic rock pose, playing bass guitar with one foot on the stack and my eyes leering at the audience.

That thing of, like, a three-piece band, you know, drums, bass and lead guitar, and they can really ROCK, you know? 'It was so LOUD, oh God, I went there and it was SO LOUD, you know, I mean it was just LOUD!' That sort of thing.

The bigger the stack the better the band. If you went to the Free Trade Hall and looked at the stage and the guitarist had four four-by-twelve cabinets, you were convinced they were going to be a great band. Why? Because they were louder than the last band you'd seen.

In this atmosphere of dedicated connoisseurship, concert audiences became as dour as those at the Royal Festival Hall. The serious fan looked askance at the loonies in the front row who waved their arms in the air, and doubly askance at anyone who had the temerity to get up and dance.

Everyone would sit round on the floor, cross-legged of course, until the band came on. If they were very boring, people would

in a broken dream

▼ Screaming Lord Sutch, looking only marginally dafter than the exemplars of early-seventies style surrounding him.

in a
broken
dream

Keith Emerson and ▶
his Moog
synthesiser,
which was as loud
as it looks.

stay sat on the floor. If not, they would generally stand and watch until the end of the number and then they'd just clap. But there was some movement towards dancing, with people generally known as the 'idiot dancers'. It involved keeping the legs rigid and just generally looning around from one leg to the other and waving their arms about as much as possible, behaving like idiots. It was quite a spectacle.

I'd judge everything by guitar solos. And if I went to a concert now and was subjected to a drum solo, I'd walk out, whereas in 1975, if I didn't hear one I wouldn't go and see that band again.

It became a cliché that every drummer sort of thrashed around for a quarter of an hour while you tried to appear a fervent fan, when actually you were bored stiff with all the clanging and the rat-tat-tatting.

Pretension in the music bred pretension in the fans; points were won or lost according to an individual's knowledge of the minutiae of the music scene, and groups, albums, musicians gained and lost 'credibility' with bewildering speed.

The aim was to be 'into' a group that nobody had ever heard of, and if you could persuade other people to like them as well, that was a bonus. Some people picked Van Der Graaf Generator for that reason.

I always remember vividly leaving school and getting on a bus and standing at bus stops, and even though it was pouring with rain you would never find my Led Zeppelin, Pink Floyd or Deep Purple albums in a bag. I'd rather have the sleeve wet and let people know what I was into. I mean, it was important to let the girls from the girls' school know that I was a weirdo and a progressive fan.

The line between progressive rock fans and devotees of disco soul music, which dominated the singles market in the early seventies, bore a remarkable resemblance to the line between the middle and working classes. An article in *New Society* in March 1973 showed that taste in music was related to academic success:

Rik Wakeman, in ▶
silver cloak, with the
150-strong cast of
'King Arthur on Ice' at
the Empire Pool,
Wembley.

The great majority of the early (school-) leavers identified themselves as 'skins' or 'smooths' and described their fellow reggae and soul fans as 'people with a bit of taste', 'people who liked to dance' and 'people who are in with the crowd'. They dismissed supporters of progressive rock as 'weirdos', 'freaks', 'scoobies' (the local derisory term for college students) and 'wankers' (that is, physically incompetent and effeminate). The academically successful pupils reciprocated by dismissing reggae fans as 'stupid skins' and 'CSE cretins'.

From these replies and subsequent conversations it was evident that pop preferences were one of the main ways through which respondents publicly signified and confirmed their subcultural identifications. Nor is this unique to our sample. A glance at the personal columns of pop music papers like *Sounds* reveals numerous ads such as 'Guy and chick seek same, into Genesis, Cohen, Tolkien. No skins, peace, ta'; or 'Scots skin wants bird, digs Slade, reggae, Tamla'.

Knowing that their brighter-than-average audience was desperate to put as much distance as possible between itself and the 'CSE cretins', the progressive groups tailored their acts accordingly. The grand became the grandiose and 'pomp rock' was born. Emerson, Lake and Palmer, who specialised in flashy rock versions of Janáček and Mussorgsky, set off on a European tour in 1973 taking with them in a convoy of trucks some twenty tons of equipment, including a custom-built proscenium arch, and a road crew of sixty. The group travelled by private plane. In the space of four weeks they played to over half a million people; there were perhaps a dozen groups in that league.

Pretension redefined itself, I think, in the early seventies. You had the advent of the synthesiser; I think particularly of Keith Emerson with a thing the size of a young telephone exchange for a medium-sized industrial town, and he used to charge around the audience with this mobile, portable ribbon-controller, wiping it on his bottom to produce the most frightful noises. And then perhaps the clown prince of them all, Rik Wakeman doing 'King Arthur on Ice' at Wembley, in this enormous silver cloak and there he was, in the middle of all these keyboards, playing . . . I suppose you could call it Radio Two ragtime music.

If you yourself, last year, had the first lasers in the country zapping around on stage and everybody saying how spectacular it was, you can't, you simply can't, do your next tour with the same stage show. You have to have not only lasers but human cannonballs.

When the Rolling Stones appeared (four hours late) at the Knebworth Festival in August 1976, they were introduced by the 'Dambusters Theme' and played off stage by a sixty-strong choir singing 'Land of Hope and Glory' while clowns and fire-eaters danced. They had a stage in the shape of an inflatable plastic mouth (Jagger danced on the tongue), and a 25,000-watt sound system. They played for two-and-three-quarter hours without performing a single new song. The triumph of form over content was complete.

And of course it was the festivals as well. Huge fields with a small stage in the distance with ridiculously pompous bands on.

It always rains at pop festivals. It's traditional. You go and sit in a puddle for a week.

The urge to recapture the spirit of Wood-stock remained, but to an increasing extent the early-seventies pop festival was a game in which very rich young men gambled vast amounts of money on the English weather. There was an aimlessness about these overblown rock jamborees, a collective feeling that only the opportunity to take drugs in the open air with relative immunity from pros-ecution made them tolerable at all.

The misuse of drugs continued and grew during the early seventies, but again it wasn't the same. LSD users, for example, reported that the drug which

in a broken dream

in 1967 had given them mystical visions and a sense of Godhead now merely scrambled their perceptions. The use of cannabis, which had originally been attended by rituals of preparation and consumption that made the Tridentine Mass look positively offhand, now became commonplace (in certain circles) and casual. The steep rise in convictions for possession of the drug (from under 5000 in 1969 to over 11,000 in 1973) partly reflects the use of new police powers under the Misuse of Drugs Act 1971, but it confirms also the widespread feeling of the time that pot really was the young person's scotch and soda.

I took a job in London with a very large insurance office. I had hair half-way down to the waist, but I had to wear a suit, so I got a suit for this and I turned up at this very large office; there must have been about a hundred people in this large, open-plan office. One chap came over and he was going to show me round. He said 'Right, that's the telex room and that's the photostat machine and there's the toilets over there and this is where we roll the joints. It you want to score any dope I do it all here . . .' And he did it all from the office, right in the heart of the city! He used to have pounds of it in his locker and he used to supply half the City of London from there. It was crazy. I started that job and after three months I had to leave because I could do the work but I couldn't cope with all the drugs. It was terrible.

▼ With this cover for *International Times*, Robert Crumb put his finger on the nub of early-seventies youth philosophy.

To the hippies' established pharmacopoeia, the early seventies added a new drug of abuse, barbiturates. Large quantities of sleeping pills, often taken with alcohol, would produce, if the patient remained (a) alive and (b) awake, the sensation which one user described as 'having your mum with you', a sort of spaced-out, laid-back, untouchable detachment. The problems of addiction and mental breakdown which resulted from this form of drug abuse were greatly underestimated (sleeping pills were very widely prescribed so how could they be dangerous?) while Press hysteria about drugs continued to focus on the much less harmful hallucinogens.

By 1972 virtually everyone who had the option of dropping back into 'straight' society had done so and the only full-time hippies left were the ageing, unemployable hard core. The students returned to their books (Genesis playing quietly in the background) and young men who had bought suits to wear as a joke now wore them as a uniform. Youth's first priority had become a decent job; the deepening recession was shrinking the middle-class employment market and limiting particularly the opportunities for the young. The proportion of the unemployed who were classed as 'school leavers and adult students' went up from 11% in 1967 to 28% in 1972.

As the hippies grew fewer, dirtier, and more disreputable, the 'straights' became more militant. In October 1971 over 80,000 young people attended a 'Festival of Light' rally in Hyde Park to hear Malcolm Muggeridge, Cliff Richard, Mary Whitehouse and Lord Longford declare war on moral pollution. The *Evening Standard* quoted a born-again baker called Robert who said: 'My life has changed completely. I've stopped drinking – I was usually as drunk as a rat by evening. I don't swear any more. I used to smoke thirty a day but I've no use for tobacco now, it's the Devil's weed.'

The *Standard* explained:

These are straight London kids. They stand opposed to pornography, extra-marital sex, adultery, abortion on social grounds, the new divorce law, homosexuality, masturbation, drugs, gambling, alcohol, tobacco, Women's Liberation and Sunday entertainments . . . They are clam-

ouring for stricter censorship, the preservation of family life and a restoration of 'traditional values'.

The best-selling record of 1972 was 'Amazing Grace' played by the band of the Royal Scots Dragoon Guards. At number two in the list of best-selling albums for the year is 'Twenty All-Time Hits of the Fifties'. Respectability ruled.

Sociologists have a useful bit of jargon in the word 'marginalisation'; it means the tendency of a society of round holes to isolate and stigmatise square pegs. It was the marginalisation of black youth in Britain that, around 1973, led to the growth of Rastafarianism. It was the marginalisation of the 'rockers', the more or less conventionally-minded motor-bike gangs of the sixties, that produced first the 'greasers' and finally the Hell's Angels.

Taking their style and rituals unchanged from the original American 'Angels', whose lineage may be traced all the way back to the early fifties, the British 'chapters' were a good deal less outrageous than the outlaw gangs of California. American Angels killed people; British ones generally confined their law-breaking to smoking pot, breaking beer glasses and riding their bikes without crash helmets. In 1971, however, a shotgun murder case and the sudden attentions of the Press turned these amiable nonconformists into the feared and hated folk devils they had aspired to be in the first place. The *People* set out to make their readers' flesh creep:

A bizarre and gruesome cult is flourishing among motor-cycle mad young men and their girlfriends in some forty British towns.

They are well-known as the Hell's Angels, but up to now almost nothing has been publicly revealed about their repellent beliefs and practices. I can now fill that gap, and millions of 'straight citizens', as cult members refer to ordinary men and women, are in for a sickening shock. For one of the Hell's Angels' principal maxims is the figure 666: it stands for sex, sin and savagery. And all three are practised by the Hell's Angels in the most nauseating form imaginable. The highest merit an

▲
One way to relieve the boredom of yet another twenty-minute guitar solo.

Angel can achieve is to perform, in public, oral sex with a woman over sixty-five years of age. Bestiality, too, is on the bravery list. So is biting the head off a live chicken ...

In real life, of course, the highest merit an Angel could achieve was to buy a round of drinks, while the 'bravery list' didn't go much further than baring one's bottom to holiday-makers on the seafront at Southend. But it suited everybody, Angels, Press and public alike, to believe that chickens cowered as the bikes roared into town. It was sad that, in the attempt to live up to their myth, some Angels committed crimes, up to and including murder, and sad too that such crimes only strengthened the legend. They remained marginal.

Just as the Hell's Angels cult was transplanted from the US to meet the needs of a marginalised group of young people, so Rastafarianism was taken dreadlock, stock and barrel from its native Jamaica to satisfy a need felt by black youth in British cities. As a fully-

*in a
broken
dream*

fledged religion, the cult of Ras Tafari, which identified Emperor Haile Selassie of Ethiopia as the returned Messiah, captured a small but significant group within the first and second generations of Caribbean immigrants to Britain. Its wider appeal was as a statement to the outside world. It implied a view of history (the 'sufferation' of black people down the ages), of world politics (their oppression by the forces of white colonial capitalism, emblematised as 'Babylon'), of black identity (stressing the qualities of dignity, being cool, 'reasoning') and of black culture (reggae music and the smoking of 'herb' or 'ganja' i.e. cannabis). It advertised itself through an instantly-identifiable appearance (long 'dreadlocks' stuffed into a knitted hat, the 'tam', in the Rasta colours of red, black, gold and green) and through a mode of speech (a thick West Indian patois, often affected, and a refusal to use the words 'me' and 'we' which were rendered as 'I' and 'I and I' respectively).

I just liked dancing to the music. The thing about political songs, sometimes you get the impression that it's just heavy and it's not there for entertainment purposes,

but with reggae it was different. You could just lay back and enjoy the music. You could tune into the words and the meanings behind it if you wanted to. You didn't have to be a Rasta, but everybody was sporting red, gold and green in some form or other, whether it was socks or bangles or earrings or jumpers or whatever. It was a way of identifying with your blackness, a positive way.

By making themselves, quite deliberately, into an identifiable anti-establishment minority within an already identifiable, oppressed minority, the Rastas courted police harrassment and too often the police obliged. Rastas became associated in the official mind with crimes of violence in general, mugging in particular, and (naturally enough) drug offences. Their street-corner life-style and their fondness for playing loud reggae late at night at rowdy parties added to their troubles with the law. It was with some surprise that the police discovered, when the inner city riots erupted in 1980 and 1981, that Rastas were the least of their problems.

**Junior Rastas in ▶
Notting Hill, 1979.
Like the Hassidic
Jews, Rastafarians
believe that the Lord
frowns upon
hair-cuts.**

popcorn

'OK, going in a car crash is fine,
but it's not like Buddy Holly dying
in a plane crash or James Dean
crashing in a sports car. Marc
Bolan died in a mini: that's
the seventies.'

popcorn

In their 1976 essay 'Beyond the Skinheads', Ian Taylor and Dave Wall describe 'the youth culture of consumer capitalism' as one which:

... celebrates existing forms as universal and inevitable, rather than particular and open to change, instrumentality (music for relaxation, dancing, and sexual conquest) rather than expressivity (music of an alternative life-style, imaginativeness or protest) and, most crucially, financial consumption rather than human participation.

It would be very easy to select from among the best-selling singles of the early seventies a list of records which would demonstrate not so much that rock'n'roll was dead as that it had never existed in the first place. This would not have mattered if the charts had been dismissed, as they were by the first-generation rock'n'rollers, as irrelevant; but now, wherever teenagers gathered to dance, at youth club, party, disco or wedding reception, the parrot cries that greeted the disc-jockey were 'Play something we know ... something in the charts ... something we can dance to.' Junior Walker and Booker T emptied the dance floor in a trice: 'Chirpy Chirpy Cheep Cheep' by Middle of the Road filled it again. The musical taste of the average fifteen-year-old had never been more corrupt; discrimination was nil; supermarkets did a roaring trade in LPs on which session singers and musicians delivered bad copies of the current Top Twenty; the Wombles were huge. The music industry had discovered that its best-selling lines were the aural equivalents of wedding cakes and tinned baby-food, so those who wanted a good square meal were driven to the junk shops in search of Phil Spector, Jerry Lee Lewis and other obscurities.

All the people that were in the charts you generally hated, you know, like Sweet and Chicory Tip and Terry Dactyl and the Dinosaurs doing that 'Seaside Shuffle' or whatever. I mean there were all sorts ... Jonathan King under every possible disguise you could imagine, wheeling out his terrible old rubbish. And we used to insist that we watched 'Top of the Pops' every week. Your father, who wanted to watch the last bit of the cricket or whatever *would be shouted down and you'd sit there all through it saying 'Oh no! Oh no-o-o! Not Demis Roussos!' and your dad would be saying 'Why the bloody hell are you watching this if you don't like any of it?'*

The most powerful force in British music was Radio One, which had set out in 1967 to replace the outlawed pirate stations. It based its daytime programming on records that were, or were thought likely to become, best-sellers. The result of this process of second-guessing popular taste by playing safe was, firstly, to produce musical stagnation (anyone who had a hit would get their follow-up played, so that would become a hit, so they'd get the follow-up played ...) and secondly, to confirm and accelerate the trend towards unadventurous and purely commercial pop music.

Moreover, because Radio One was unwilling to alienate the housewife listener, it programmed music that was least likely to make anyone actually switch off. This of course, meant excluding an awful lot of the music that was most likely to make some people turn up the volume.

John Walters, who produced a late-evening programme in which more interesting music was allowed air-time, remarked (in a Radio Four interview):

Radio One is creating a market for records which are only suitable for Radio One, in the sense that companies are tempted to produce something like 'Sugar Sugar', 'Knock three times on the ceiling if you want me' kind of records, which a producer will listen to and say 'Great. That's a Radio One record, it's short, bright, bouncy ...'

Music was now far removed from the control of the teenagers: they would buy what they were given and like it; the idea of their attempting to buy instruments and sound like either Deep Purple on the one hand or Lynsey de Paul on the other was quite ludicrous. In the same way, the other elements of youth culture, such as venues, magazines and clothing fashions, were gradually being standardised and marketed in a way that effectively removed the possibility of

consumer choice. Do-it-yourself was not an option.

In cities, where there had once been a variety of cheap, separately-owned cellar clubs catering for different clienteles, there were now large, glossy discotheques and chicken-in-the-basket palaces owned by national concerns like Bailey's, Fiesta and Top Rank, which brought a Butlins flavour to the teens-and-twenties night out. The survival of the 'Northern soul' tradition at the Wigan Casino and similar venues was evidence that the kids still wanted their own private culture based on dance and music; but for every disco in which athletic lads in baggy trousers did the splits to sixties soul records of the utmost obscurity, there were a hundred in which bored, blank-faced girls in hot-pants shuffled round their handbags to the sound of Tony Christie.

Girls always used to wear the same clothes and they always used to dance the same at discos. They also used to have these square handbags that looked like little suitcases, often made out of patent leather, and they used to carry them sort of on their wrist. But when they danced in groups they used to take their shoes off, I suppose for comfort, and then they'd put these little suitcase handbags down on the floor and dance round them, or sometimes they'd dance in lines, and they'd all do exactly the same thing, and there was great pleasure in all doing the same thing and not having any quirk. You know, nobody was trying to be different at all.

We didn't do anything except dance and pose about. We didn't think about anything or even discuss or care about anything, you know, politically or anything like that. But on the other hand, at that time we did become more involved with coloured people at discos where they played soul music, and perhaps we became more aware of them and some of the difficulties they had getting into clubs and things like that.

If any discos allowed any trousers at all for girls they had to be white, because it went with the fluorescent lights you see, and everybody was going 'Oh look at her, she's got a speck on her trousers!' Everything had to be white. It was a very clean image.

A particular kind of soul music, which bore the same relation to James Brown and Otis Redding as processed cheese to Gorgonzola, was supplied for disco consumption. The Stylistics, Chi-lites, Al Green and Barry White led the way, to be followed later in the decade by the synthesised pulsations of Donna Summer, Boney M (both, significantly enough, produced in Germany), Gloria Gaynor and the Three Degrees. In the end it turned out that the group who churned out disco soul most successfully, the Bee Gees, were white.

Just as the Top Rank Suite replaced the Heaven and Hell Club, so the 'Man About Town' and 'Teen Miss' departments of the high-street stores replaced the boutiques (those that survived went way up-market). As the aftermath of hippie fashion merged with the new chain-store trendiness, some peculiar combinations of clothing appeared on the streets.

Around about '71 my brother got married. If you look back at his wedding photos, you see he had the platform shoes, he had the silly hair, bright checked jacket, green shirt and dark red velvet bow tie. God knows what he was wearing for trousers. He'd run out of things to make clash with it really. He'll forgive me for saying this, but he looks a sight.

Loon pants! You know, people used to boast about how wide their trousers were round the bottom. They were hipster loons and they were advertised on the back of Sounds magazine with this drooping figure with drooping hair and these drooping loon pant trousers.

Platform soles! I had these brilliant blue platforms, just five-inch-high blocks of wood that had huge great brass studs on the side and leather over the top of them, and I used to stagger round on those.

Tank tops! What you'd now call a sleeveless pullover, but then it was called a tank top. They had stripes on them and in fact I knitted one myself. In fact it was the first garment I ever managed to knit for myself and get even tension and get the ribbing proper on the bottom. I felt really proud of that, but I'm sure it isn't cool for skinheads to be proud of something that they've knitted themselves.

popcorn

popcorn

We used to wear Indian sort of embroidered smock-tops, and we used to go to C & A and buy these horrible long cardigans.

I remember I got a Crimplene trouser-suit as a present for passing my Eleven-plus, and when hotpants came in, my mother cut down the Crimplene trousers and made a pair of hotpants. Now at that stage I was still in my chubby phase and they must have looked the pits. I mean, you know, what a cruel fashion! Awful. And those awful wet-look boots that had elastic round the tops and cut off all the circulation to your feet, and they were plastic and you used to hear these dreadful horror stories of people standing too near the fire and their boots would melt into their skin and they'd have to have skin grafts.

The liberal display of female flesh that was afforded by see-through blouses, short skirts and hotpants was more of a tease than a promise; frustrated, fumbling lads looked back wistfully to the days of loose skirts and stockings. In fact the pendulum of permissiveness, which had been moving towards 'anything goes' during the late sixties, was now swinging back again, while the double standard remained firmly in place. For a 1971 radio programme on 'The Permissive Society' a reporter brought back this intelligence from the sexual battlefront:

Girl: I agree with not sleeping around with people but, you know, when you're going to get married and you're engaged and everything, it's different then. If you feel that way about each other, well why not?
Boy: I've been out with one or two who'd just go to bed with anybody.
–And what do you think about that?
–Well, it's their problem really. Nothing to do with me. If a girl will sleep around with anybody I mean she's naturally branded as a slag, but I don't believe there is such a word myself. I mean if she likes sex, that's fair enough.
–But you wouldn't like to marry one?
–Oh no, of course not.

People had parties which were such dens of iniquity really. People lying around groping on the floor because it was the only chance they had, and people's parents coming home and finding other people on their bed. Oh dear . . . I can remember sitting in a flower bed at somebody's party, you know, alternately throwing up and kissing somebody, I mean, he didn't seem to mind at all. It was all very tacky. I don't know that there's any getting away from the fact that being a teenager is really a very tacky sort of time.

One observation on which everyone seemed to agree was that girls were now growing up faster than they ever had before. At an age at which their mothers had dreamed of ponies and Brownie revels, they were buying romance magazines, lipstick and junior bras and dreaming of Donny Osmond. The difference cannot entirely be ascribed to a gradual lowering of the age of puberty; it had rather more to do with the identification by commercial interests of another potentially lucrative market, the pre-teens. The Beatles, by attracting much younger fans than previous pop stars, had pointed the way. The Monkees, a group cynically assembled to appeal to that market, had demonstrated that the proposition was viable. Now the record companies launched into mass production, turning out clean, pretty young men who were, above all, as sexually unthreatening as teddy bears. The result surprised even those who had planned it; in October 1973 the *Daily Telegraph* reported:

Screams of adulation turned to screams of panic when part of a parapet collapsed and fell on the heads of hundreds of youngsters – 'weenyboppers' – welcoming the American Osmond Brothers pop group at Heathrow yesterday. A senior policeman said: 'There is always hysteria with these youngsters. I cannot understand the mentality of parents who allow children to travel unaccompanied all over the country just to scream at an airport or station.'

We were just a lot of emotional nutcases when you look back on it, because we were either screaming or shouting for our

favourite pop group, or standing there after they'd gone saying 'Oh I love him, I wish he'd come back' and 'He's mine, not yours'. And it was just what it said – 'teenybopper' – bopping about either crying or screaming or shouting or something like that.

I was in a classroom at school, and these girls had magazines and they were looking through them and there was a picture of David Cassidy in the shape of a heart, and I said 'Cor, who's he?', you know, and that was it. From that moment onwards I wouldn't let go of it. I thought 'That's it! I've got to find out more about this fella definitely.'

We bought T-shirts and badges and posters, you know, the whole lot. I used to collect everything I could find about him, or as much as I could afford – as much as my mum could afford. I used to know all sorts of tiny details like what kind of food he liked, the names of his dogs, even down to his ring size ...

When David Cassidy sang 'I Think I Love You', he used to point his finger in the middle of the song. There was many a time I was convinced that he'd perhaps pointed at me. I wondered if he'd ever remember my face if I ever met up with him. It was a very strange feeling because you were in a world of your own despite the fact that there were thousands of people round you, screaming their heads off.

I remember one night on the radio there was a big announcement that there was a really strong rumour that he'd got married, and I came haring down the stairs in tears and my mum said to me 'Don't be silly, you'll grow out of it'. I said 'I'll never grow out of it. I don't want to live any more!' It was a miserable two days until somebody confirmed that it wasn't true.

The first British act to be sold in a big way to the teenybop market was an Edinburgh group which had started life in 1967 as the Saxons. A smart manager called Tam Paton stuck a pin in a map of America, hit Bay City, Michigan and called his group the Bay City Rollers. He dressed them in short, baggy, white trousers trimmed with tartan, gave them

popcorn

◄ **David Cassidy gives his all ...**

▼ **... and the fans react. At this concert at White City in May 1974, a fourteen-year-old girl suffered cardiac arrest.**

123

popcorn

some bubblegum tunes and some sessionmen to play on the records, and cleaned up.

The first concert I went to, to be quite honest, was just a very frightening experience because I didn't know kids went so hysterical. They were falling off balconies, falling off seats and getting trampled on . . .

▲ **Tartan-clad Roller fans express their appreciation of the group's musical talent.**

After a Rollers concert at the Hammersmith Odeon in June 1975, thirty fans ended up in hospital, some with fractured ribs and some with asphyxia. The man from the St John's Ambulance blamed the group for enticing the girls to come forward in the hope of a kiss.

Unlike the Osmond and Cassidy fans, who had settled for scarves and badges, the Roller fans had a full-dress uniform; they dressed and styled their hair exactly like the group, so that one was hard put to say, seeing both performers and fans, which looked sillier.

In the gangs, you used to wear something to identify yourself by. I suppose you could call it a fashion, but at the time we didn't consider it fashion, we just lived it. We were all in a gang and we were rivals

against the Bay City Rollers fans. As soon as you saw any tartan scarves around, or half-mast pants with tartan on them you'd shout ' There's a Rollers fan!' and we were after them . . .

Even stranger than the sight of dozens of pubescent girls bouncing through the streets dressed like escaped clowns from a Scottish circus was the appearance of the audience at a Gary Glitter concert. As he recalled in a radio interview:

When I did the Palladium the kids with the glitter in their hair and the make-up and the whole thing, it was a little bit wild. I mean, this was 1972 . . . A lot of the kids used to arrive with a little suitcase, go into the loo at the Palladium, get the gear out and put the make-up on and the glitter in their hair and so on, just for the occasion, then afterwards they'd go back in the loo and wash it all off and go home and say 'Hey, Mummy and Daddy, I'm really only a sweet little child . . .'

Stranger still was the man himself; a revenant (like Alvin Stardust, formerly Shane Fenton) from a previous incarnation as a rock'n'roller when his name had been Paul Raven, he literally dazzled the teenyboppers by dressing like a cross between a Flash Gordon villain and a pantomime dame, bawling playground chants over a stormtrooper backing.

It was the glitter! It was people like Gary Glitter who decided to use the stage like it should be used! That's what excited me. To get up and use his face and use his clothes and his expressions – to me that was so brilliant. He got up on that stage and showed you how to dress in glitter gear, right down to his boots. I mean even his boots weren't just platform boots, they were covered with glitter! I thought it would be marvellous to have the guts to get up on stage and dress like that.

'Glitter rock' was the teenybop end of a bigger movement which became known as 'glam rock'. Like Gary Glitter and Alvin Stardust, Marc Bolan and David Bowie were make-overs from earlier

popcorn

periods of pop music. Both had been playing in bands in the late sixties, and had come through the effeminate aftermath of the mod period. Now they journeyed on through high camp to the very edge of out-and-out transvestism.

Bolan, the 'bopping elf' of Tyrannosaurus Rex, shortened the name of his group to T Rex and scored a remarkable number of hits with minor variations of the same sound – a weedy warble laid on top of a thumping metronomic beat.

Marc Bolan actually set the flavour, such as it was; a fairly bland flavour I think. The glitter was disguising the fact that there was nothing really new underneath, because a lot of his music was just old rock'n'roll retreads, wasn't it? They were just old rock riffs – nothing to it. 'Girl I'm just a jeepster for your love' ... Very nice. What does it mean?

Both musically and culturally, Bowie was a more interesting phenomenon. Essentially a singer-songwriter in the post-Dylan tradition, he unified the pretension of the early-seventies avant-garde (a dash of Andy Warhol, a sprinkle of science fiction, a cut-up writing technique borrowed from William Burroughs) with the theatricality of the pantomime school of rock performers. It was cynical, of course, but cynicism was part of the pose. Taylor and Wall, in their perceptive essay on glam rock, argue that 'Bowie's acceptability seems to lie precisely in his ability to play back the youth culture's own awareness of exploitation and emptiness.' They quote Bowie himself:

At least part of me is saying what a load of rubbish the whole rock business is and what a load is written about it. And if I can tart it up enough maybe people will see that it has a lot to do with them. We're not the great thinkers of our time, as you might believe from all the interviews we have to do. We're as close to real thinking as Mary Whitehouse, just as naïve and bigoted.

Bowie's dominance of the mid-seventies was made possible because he appealed to his audience on many

levels. Posing as a neutered alien, he had the sexlessness that attracted the pre-teen female (on the inner cover of his 'Aladdin Sane' LP he was, as *Rolling Stone* delicately put it, 'airbrushed into androgyny'). He was a fashion-plate for the mid-teens: every time he changed his outfit (he re-styled himself for every album and every concert tour), the look-alikes, both male and female, rushed back to their wardrobes and their make-up boxes and followed suit. Finally, he achieved credibility with the university crowd by delivering apocalyptic lyrics in a cracked, world-weary voice which distanced him from his own 'stardom'. The real Bowie, he implied, was very different from his stage personae. All this was much too subtle for the *Sun,* which in May 1973 gave him the tabloid treatment:

WOWIE! This man David Bowie is the Pied Piper of the new fun fashion rebellion. He's doing for fashion (and make-up) what the Beatles did just ten years ago. And 18,000 excited fans dressed up for the big David

▼ **Bisexual chic: David Bowie at his campest in October 1973.**

Bowie pop show at London's Earls Court this weekend to prove the Bowie wave has arrived. Many wore the full Bowie bit. Hair short and tufty, coloured and feathered. Make-up was chalk white with the Bowie trade-mark gash of lightning across the face in red and blue. Glitter jackets were worn with drain-pipe pants. And David's own new face mark was a large glitter spot in the centre of his forehead.

Sexual ambiguity was chic in these years. The air was full of gruff voices on radio phone-ins complaining that these days the only way you could tell boys from girls was by looking for the bust.

Or, as a twelve-year-old Bowie fan put it: 'I think his dress is a bit ladylike. I think he'd look better with trousers on.'

When I started going out with the big love of my teenage life, I used to go to these dances at the local rugby club, and the one I really went for was this guy who wore green eye shadow to a rugby club dance. I thought he was frightfully good stuff.

▼ The Hammersmith Odeon, July 1973, and Bowie fans appear with look-alike facial paint-jobs.

While the pop world flirted with decadence in this fin de siècle fashion (Bowie, inevitably, was a keen collector of Third Reich memorabilia), the real world was becoming bleaker by the day.

Unemployment was then a million when I left school and was trying to get a job for the first time, and we thought this was shocking, absolutely shocking.

I was catching bits and pieces on the news, and at school as well we started to get cutbacks in the library and we started to feel little things like that. It did worry me, although I did think I would end up with a job. I never thought that when I reached the end of my teens I wouldn't have a job, which was the case as it turned out. But I didn't envisage it like that at all.

I really think we were the last generation before the recession. In the sixties things were so comfortable and easy for people and everything was expanding and there were new things all the time. That was slowing down during my teens, and it stopped more or less when my teens stopped. I just feel I was lucky to get through. They wouldn't admit me to university now, on the A-level grades I got. I was just lucky to get through the gate before they shut it off.

A *Sunday Times* feature writer in June 1975 was among the first to suggest that teenage culture had shot its bolt:

Whatever happened to the kids? Mods, rockers, beatniks, greasers, flower-children, hippies – you could depend on them to start things up.

How, the writer worried, would retired Rear Admirals spend their time, now that there was no longer any cause for them to write outraged letters to the *Daily Telegraph*?

The answer was just around the corner.

pretty vacant

'Oh, good old pogo-ing. Great.
Jumping up and down on top
of people. Spitting at the band,
that was de rigueur. Just like eels,
like eels wriggling about in a bucket.'

pretty vacant

I do remember punk like nothing else. Everything else was just a fashion, but that was something else.

I was sixteen and I hadn't really been a teenager yet and rebelled and been wild, which is what kids are supposed to do. I thought 'Perhaps this is it, perhaps that's all there is to it. A few nice LPs and the NME every Wednesday and that's youth.' But suddenly this happened and, you know, you wanted to be offensive. You wanted to upset people.

Punk brought together a style of music that had evolved in the US, a style of dress that came from the London arty avant-garde and a philosophy that came from the streets. It was acutely self-conscious, the first authentic teenage revolt to be chronicled and dissected by its own trendsetters *while it was happening*. It was full of paradox: a synthesis of puritanism and anarchy; avowedly anti-intellectual yet tireless in its efforts to analyse itself, its ideas, its antecedents, its symbolism; determined that there would be 'no leaders', yet ever ready to follow anyone who seemed to know what was going on. Above all, it was a genuine if short-lived revolution, in which teenagers recaptured their own culture through do-it-yourself fashion, music, concerts, record-production and magazines.

There is a very simple explanation of punk which, although it begs more questions than it answers, is nevertheless important because it is what most punks believed they were all about. It goes like this: between 1974 and 1976 the rate of unemployment rose from 2.6% to 5.7%, with young people the worst-hit group. At some point along the way, the number of kids who saw themselves as having no future in 'straight' society reached critical mass, and developed a collective attitude which refused to accept the equation 'unemployment equals failure'. 'If society doesn't need us', they said, 'we don't need society; if they deny us employment, respect and rewards, we shall make ourselves as unemployable and unrespectable as we can, and we shall reward ourselves in ways society does not understand; we shall find our pride in the very fact of our worthlessness.'

At the heart of this rationale there was a dishonesty. 'We don't care what people think of us', they proclaimed, loudly and often. But it wasn't true. Punks' central preoccupation was what people thought of them. They simply said to society what teenagers had said to their parents from the beginning: 'Now look what you've made me do!' They set out, quite consciously, to be a living reproach, a spectre at the feast. Without the shock and outrage there would have been very little point.

The slogan of punk, ▶ used in a Sex Pistols lyric: 'No future' . . .

In 1971 an ex-art student called Malcolm McLaren and an ex-teacher called Vivienne Westwood opened a shop at 430, King's Road, Chelsea, selling Teddy boy clothes to a small but dedicated clique of fifties revivalists. They called their boutique 'Let It Rock' and the chemist next door complained about the noise from the juke-box. In 1974 they changed the name to 'Too Fast to Live, Too Young to Die' and started selling leather gear to rockers. By 1975 they had changed again; this time the boutique was called 'Sex' and the stock consisted of offensively rude T-shirts, rubberwear and bondage trousers tied together at the knee. They employed a sales assistant called Jordan Hook who wore plastic leotards, a black suspender belt and thigh boots, but styled her hair and painted her face to look like a corpse that had spent some time on a rubbish dump. The aim was not to look sexy, it was to disgust people; in fact it was a 'statement', and what it said was something like: 'You thought this kind of gear was sexy, you filthy old pervert? I'll wear it and make you puke and then maybe you'll realise that teenage girls are not on this planet for middle-aged wankers to drool over.' The art students loved it.

By the autumn of '76 the glam rock decadence that had dominated the London art-school fashion scene was changing rapidly under the influence of this new 'Let's be disgusting' style of chic. *New Society* described the look:

Their hair is cut close to the bone, often dyed bizarre colours. Make-up is worn by both sexes: white faces, blue lips and green eye-shadow suggest the appearance of puppyfat refugees from a Venusian cabaret.

Some wear black vinyl or seethrough black fishnet vests. Drainpipe lurex trousers and stilettoheeled shoes are popular with the girls, while the boys wear shirts with the arms torn off at the shoulder, or T-shirts slashed as if with knifethrusts. Body jewellery includes leather straps, chains, razor-blade pendants (implying the use of cocaine), and earrings in the shape of scissors. The overall impression is of Clockwork Orange meets New York sado-masochism with just a hint of Weimar.

Many of those who dressed in the parody-of-porn style described here would have understood that last sentence; some of them could have written a ten-page critique of it; maybe they did. But as punk style spread, its exponents forgot where it had come from and worried instead about where it was going.

Fashion at the time was basically just to wear anything that would shock or outrage. Girls would go around with zips across their chests, undo them and show a large amount of bosom, which absolutely shocked the grandmothers.

One thing I did crave after was plastic sandals. I went everywhere to get plastic sandals and in the end I got a pair and they were beautiful. They were a kind of nicotine plastic and they're horrible. I love them.

There were certain ways of looking horrible. I mean, you could tell the ones who looked good and horrible and those who just looked horrible. They had no idea, basically. And you could be obnoxious and rude, you know, and throwing up in public places was not unheard of – just upsetting grannies and worrying people, but never really confronting major problems of the day with your dress or anything. Yeah, you couldn't get into clubs or pubs, you just generally were thrown out, and by being thrown out like that you did link up with more people and become a bigger group and a stronger group. It was all very incestuous.

When people wore swastikas, I think that was more to shock than because of any racist overtone. The time when Sid Vicious went round a Jewish area in France wearing a swastika T-shirt, just to shock and outrage all the people there, I thought that was going beyond whatever line you shouldn't go beyond.

Oh I had a very fetching hair-style. I had a quarter-inch crop all over, and a long straggly blonde fringe which lent itself very well to food colouring, so that one could choose one's fringe according to one's outfit. One could use strawberry food colouring, green food colouring or whatever. Or all of them. And what was best about my hair-cut was that it made me look so awful. My mother wouldn't walk down the street with me. I think I liked that idea.

▲ **The Rainbow, May 1977: a classic example of the much-favoured tongue-out-and-roll-your-eyes pose.**

pretty vacant

Discovering the best way of making your hair stand on end was one of the best-kept secrets of punk. You tried everything – sugar, toothpaste, glue, soap, washing-up liquid, cooking oil, lard, butter ... It was before the mass-production of hair gels, you see. That was another thing to come out of punk rock – hair gel!

Every teenage culture consists of a wide circle of people who look the part surrounding a much smaller circle who live the part, so just as there had been weekend ravers and weekend hippies, there were now weekend punks. It wasn't only a matter of dress and hair-style; there was a punk way of speaking, a clipped, consonantal, smirking tone, very heavy on the t's, n's and r's. To hear a punk pronounce the word 'Crimplene' was to feel the very texture of the cloth.

Everybody was calling themselves punk. Everybody was like me. They put on a pair of tight trousers and their dad's jacket, three sizes too big, and their grandad's raincoat and a pair of fluorescent socks and started masquerading as a punk.

We were all weekend punks. We were all very clean punks. We didn't go round spitting. We certainly didn't wear razor-blades hanging from our ears, it would have been dangerous! But we wore very clean sponge-down vinyl trousers and very expensive loose-knit mohair jumpers in acidic colours – lime green preferably – and very tastefully-ripped tee-shirts with very carefully-written expletives over them. But it was all very contrived.

There was a strange kind of snobbery. You'd refer to people as weekend punks, the ones that wore very expensive punk clothing. I was rather snobby about that. They were just following fashion, they weren't real punks. Real punks were people with no money who drank cider. I was more impressed by bright orange Crimplene and horrible fabrics and disgusting bad-taste clothes which actually poked fun at the people like parents who actually wore these Crimplene clothes in all seriousness. You'd wear them and turn it around on them, which laughed at them. I think punk had a lot of humour which people missed. It was a lot of poking

fun and winding people up and laughing at them, and if they reacted with anger it made it even better, because that was exactly what you wanted authority to do.

The first blast of press publicity for the cult came at the beginning of December 1976. The *Daily Mail* called punk rock 'the sickest, seediest step in a rock world that thought it had seen it all'. The *Daily Mirror* stressed the themes of violence, self-mutilation and sex:

They dance to songs that preach destruction ... devotion to the cult means wearing safety-pins through their nostrils ... Other punk hallmarks include swastikas and hairstyles that look as though they have been created with carving knives ... Punk rock girls, with lips painted black, are just as startling. Their outfits include shocking-coloured tights with just a G-string over them, and T-shirts with zips over the boobs.

The following day the *Mirror* returned to the attack: 'Who are these punks? They wear torn and ragged clothes held together with safety pins. They are boorish, ill-mannered, foul-mouthed, dirty, obnoxious and arrogant. They like to be disliked.' Again, the paper was particularly fascinated by those safety pins 'through their ears, noses or even their cheeks'.

Nah, there was ways of getting round that. You can get a safety pin and by bending the hook piece back on itself you can make it appear to go through your cheek and out the other side.

Self-mutilation was a very important part of punk. There were all the tattoos that went with it, girls going out and being tattooed as never before ... people being tattooed on their head and on their neck, and not just saying 'I love Mother' but saying other things ...

Oh it was hilarious really. We were in London, just walking down Oxford Street, and we got these Jehovah's Witnesses coming up to us and they told us that punk was sinister and evil and all that, and we

said 'What makes you say that?'. 'Oh, we've read it in the Sunday papers' ... And all the hyperbole in the Sunday papers was absolutely ridiculous. I think that encouraged punk more than anything.

Everybody knows about the famous Bill Grundy episode. I mean, he was goading them on to say the words he wanted them to say, they said it; he got a rollocking for it and they got the front page.

In fact it was the 'Grundy episode' that started the furore. In the course of an interview with the Sex Pistols (of whom more anon) in Thames Television's regional news programme 'Today' on 1 December, the group had been invited to be outrageous and had obliged with the most outrageous words they could think of, which shocked some but did not surprise many. Grundy was suspended for two weeks, a viewer rang to say he had kicked in the screen of his new television, a delegation from the Transport and General Workers' Union asked EMI Records to cancel their contract with the Sex Pistols and the *Daily Mirror* launched a competition for the worst punk jokes (sample: 'What is pink, sickly and has a four-letter word all the way through it? – Punk rock.')

Punk rock did indeed have four-letter words all the way through it, but there was more to it than that. Its musical antecedents were almost all American During the sixties, the popularity of British groups in the US had inspired a rash of imitative 'garage bands' such as the Shadows of Knight, the Standells and the MC5. Their music, simplistic but energetic, came back into vogue in the late seventies as an antidote to pomp rock.

They were the first groups to attract the label 'punk rock'. During the seventies, an East Coast minimalist school of rock'n'roll had developed. Inability to sing had come to be regarded as a virtue, and indeed had failed to prevent the likes of Patti Smith and Jonathan Richman from making some charming, simple pop records.

At the same time, the decadent wing of American 'schlock-rock' had taken outrage on stage about as far as it could manage. Iggy Pop, of Iggy and the Stooges, regularly stripped off, cut himself with broken glass and fell into

the front row of the audience. The New York Dolls were a transvestite band who worked hard at untuning their guitars before every performance (the ubiquitous Malcolm McLaren had been their manager for a while).

The third ingredient was supplied by such groups as Richard Hell and the Voidoids and, above all, the Ramones, who delivered loud, fast, simple songs that lasted no more than two minutes and celebrated the joys of headbanging, sniffing glue and being extremely stupid.

While the seed of punk rock was germinating in the US the soil was being prepared for its transplantation to London. Two developments in particular fertilised the ground: pub rock and 'indie' record companies.

By the mid-seventies, the cost to the major record companies of launching a new band had become prohibitive. The money-spinners were the established 'name bands' who, as tax exiles, hardly ever performed in the UK (and if they did charged £10 for the privilege of watching them through binoculars from a quarter of a mile away). Not only could up-and-coming bands not get a record contract, they were hard put to find a place to play. The clubs had been replaced by discos, and the only places that featured live music on a regular basis were the college social clubs and a few pubs.

pretty vacant

▼ **The Sex Pistols' 1978 line-up (left to right): Sid Vicious, Johnny Rotten, Steve Jones. The drummer was Paul Cook.**

pretty vacant

All these groups started opening up in back rooms of pubs and clubs, and a lot of awful groups, but that wasn't the point. It was just good fun going out and making a noise, and you were the people doing it, it wasn't somebody signed to EMI or CBS, it was someone you went to school with or who worked in a garage or whatever. It was you helping to organise it and they were your friends up on stage and you knew 90% of the audience and you knew all the people you were upsetting who worked behind the bar, and it was great.

Musically, the pub rock bands weren't very interesting. They reworked old rock'n'roll and rhythm'n'blues standards and wrote new songs in the same tradition. The best of them did graduate to making records, only a few of which were noticed. But out of this random assortment of frustrated talents came the demand for small, flexible record companies that could operate on the cheap, selling simply-produced records in modest numbers to loyal, local fan followings. The 'indies' saw the need and set out to meet it. Moreover, because they had their ears closer to the ground, independent companies like Stiff and Chiswick spotted winners the majors missed and signed up a few hit-makers along with the no-hopers. When punk rock arrived and the major companies turned up their noses, the 'indies' became very important indeed.

Grassroots rock'n'roll had all but died in the shadow of the supergroups. What was needed to start the whole process going again was a seventies equivalent of skiffle, and that's what punk rock was.

As soon as I heard the music, you know, I took off on that straight away. The other records were sort of discarded and I picked up the guitar again. I did pick one up in the early seventies and I found that, because I couldn't play like Eric Clapton in a few weeks, you know, I gave up. But punk and all that really gave me a new enthusiasm to start playing again. Within a couple of years I was out playing with groups in just small little halls. I just really enjoyed it. It was a great time. Little promoters and halls and a demand to come and watch anyone getting up on stage and playing something new and something exciting and

something very easy as well. You know, every block was starting to do it.

In the days of elitism, if your guitar was out of tune you used to get really embarrassed in your guitar solo, yet there were all these kids that didn't even know how to tune their guitars. They bought it in the shop and just presumed it was all right from the day they bought it or stole it or whatever to the day they performed with it in front of 700 or more people; then the chances were you'd throw it into the audience anyway so it didn't really matter. If you went home with it at the end of the night, that was a bonus.

Britain's first exclusively punk venue, the Roxy, in Covent Garden, opened on New Year's Day 1977. Between January and April, when the promoter was ejected for failing to pay the rent, it witnessed unprecedented scenes.

A group of us from round here decided to go to this big do. It was the Clash were playing, opening up the Roxy. Oh it was excellent. You just got in there and there were all these punks and freakos. It was a whole new scene and yet you felt really part of it. You felt that you were something, you were something different.

You were just part of the mass that was swirling around and going up and down and it was hot and sweaty and the music was relentless.

I actually remember sitting at the back on my own, feeling very frightened and threatened by this mad noise. It just blew my head actually.

The combination of loud, aggressive music, a determination to flout such conventions of concert etiquette as respecting other people's 'personal space', and the prevalence of amphetamines (the punk drug), produced a pattern of audience behaviour that had to be seen to be believed. Crammed together in front of the stage, the fans had no room to dance so they 'pogo-ed'.

Pogo-ing was very violent and very painful. People were not quite crushed to death, but serious injuries occurred. If

you've got a hundred people all jumping up and down very frenetically together, you're going to get people hurt, and that was part of it. I was frightened of pogoing except with people that I knew well, because it was dangerous. Yes, performers leaping off the stage into the crowd and glasses being thrown and instruments being thrown. It was all very violent and very dangerous, and that's why I think it was so attractive to people.

People actually got up on stage and were singing with the actual performers and were pogo-ing up and down with them. We were with them!

Apparently the origin of spitting at gigs came from an early Damned gig at which somebody threw a can of beer at Rat Scabies and he just went up to the bloke, pulled him up by the scruff of his neck and spat in his face. From then on everybody decided spitting was a good idea. Yeah, it was certainly a ruck and everyone was certainly bashing into each other and having a good old time being energetic and throwing things about, but I don't think it was ever sinister aggression. But then the papers got hold of it and claimed it was sinister.

The second wave of press outrage broke in the summer of 1977 after a series of violent incidents at punk concerts such as the major Clash appearance at the Rainbow in May when 200 seats were smashed. As concert halls throughout the land issued statements to the effect that punk groups were banned, the newspapers rummaged through punk for ever more lurid tales of depravity. In August the *News of the World* produced a classic:

'HOW HELEN LED HER SCHOOLBOY SON INTO THE SICK WORLD OF PUNK ROCKERS'

I'm glad Mrs Helen Relfe, thirty-five, is a mum in a million. Because I wouldn't like to think there are many more like her. She is bringing up her son Roger, fifteen, to be a punk rock star. She persuaded him to call himself Dee Generate. And she is delighted that he lives up to the name...

Mrs Relfe was really knocked out by her son's sickening antics on stage... like faking a bleeding mouth during a performance by biting on the sort of blood capsule used by film

▼The Clash on stage at the Roxy. Note the chord-letters marked on Paul Simenon's bass guitar.

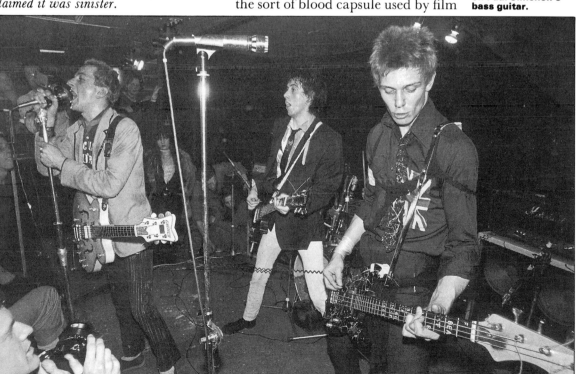

pretty vacant

stuntmen. 'They used to shriek at that', Mum said. But she thought twice about Dee's most gruesome stunt. A pig's head was ceremoniously carried on stage with a safety pin through its nose. Then, while the rest of the group played, Dee hacked it to pieces in a frenzy with a chopper and a hammer. 'I did think it might be carrying it too far', said Mrs Relfe. 'But Dee was quite right. It was fantastic.' Dee added: 'It was good all right. I'd sawed its head up a bit so the brains would spill out more easily. When the eyes shot out into the audience the fans went berserk.'

For a more sympathetic account of the scene, punks went to their own organs of communication, the fanzines.

Fanzines were the result of a combination of speed and polytechnics. When you get intelligent working-class kids using amphetamines, you don't get any lessening

▼ **Issue one (and only) of a typical fanzine.**

of the intelligence but what you do get is an obsessive determination to analyse everything down to the last dot and comma, and a lot of energy to get on and do it.

Credit for starting the first punk fanzine is usually accorded to Mark Perry, an unemployed teenager from Deptford, who launched *Sniffin' Glue* in the late summer of 1976. By the following summer it was selling 8000 copies every time it made its irregular appearance, and it had produced literally hundreds of imitators.

If you could play one chord you could form a pop group; if you could write two sentences you could start a fanzine. I mean, loads of people did it at schools, at colleges, at the library or whatever. You just got twenty A4 sheets, cut out any ridiculous pictures you could and made montages. People spent hours cutting out pictures of the Queen's head and sticking it onto monsters' bodies, all of it clichéd stuff but great fun; you know, silly patterns and writing upside down and at odd angles and cut-out lettering, you know, blackmail letter stuff. It was great. Everyone thought they were famous for the fifteen minutes they'd been promised, and for fifteen minutes they were. No-one remembers them now of course.

I do remember them but I had no great interest in them because the music papers were so good then. Everyone had to read NME because, as far as I'm concerned, it made punk anyway. We had good old Julie Burchill, the voice of a generation.

Julie Burchill and Tony Parsons, two bright and fluent teenagers, had been hired by the *New Musical Express* in 1976 to explain to the readership, and more importantly to the ageing hippies on the paper's editorial staff, what the hell was going on. They proceeded to change the character of the journal completely, elevating themselves in the process to the roles of head gurus, advisers and chroniclers to the punk movement. Burchill's weekly despatches, piling generalisation upon denunciation and insight upon sneer, gave punk whatever it had in the way of a self-conscious philosophy. It was, she said, a feminist movement:

(No!) KILL IT.

For Snuffing glue freaks.

Interview:
Sue. E. Side →
of Bristols Diggers.

alberto y lost trios paranoias

Interview:
Wolf Frenzy →

Contents:—
Exclusive interviews with
Exciting revalations from beyond.
Dead good pictures that have rocked the world of showbiz.
We try and answer the question : Huh ?
Original programme notes for "Razorblades and Roundshot."

hundreds of dead people

X. RATING :- FOR IDIOTS ONLY.

Punk in 1976 was the first rock'n'roll phase *ever* not to insist that women should be picturesque topics and targets of songs ... Blessed with the finest imagination of her generation, Poly Styrene (born Marion Elliott) has disregarded her social handicaps (race, sex and class) which anyone else would have built a career around ...

And it was true that never before had the lead singer of a rock'n'roll band appeared with braces on her teeth and prompted her fans to insist that *that was the point.*

If you're talking about a philosophy of punk, the philosophy is anarchical and self-destructive and nihilistic and all those long words, innit? But when I was doing it, I did it purely because I wanted to be noticed, and when you're about sixteen you want an identity, don't you? Because society doesn't give you one, or doesn't give you the chance to develop one. You're just part of the system – I'm talking about people who've gone to comprehensive schools and really big schools where you're sort of like a sausage in a sausage machine. They turn you out, grind you out, year by year. So you're looking for something a bit different.

At its irreducible simplest, punk philosophy was a mere inversion of hippie philosophy. In place of 'Love and Peace', Joe Strummer wrote on the back of his jacket 'Hate and War'.

Some of the hippies actually quite liked punk. They used to come up and say 'Hey man, society's rejected our love and peace philosophy, now they've got your hate and violence philosophy. Right on!' We'd just say 'Yeah, it's good, innit?'

The spirit of punk was aggressive, certainly, but it was a spirit of rejection rather than destruction. It rejected, in particular, the view of society implied by the mid-seventies' consensus politics which informed the media.

Someone said to me that until punk rock happened they used to be quite happy to read the 'Daily Mail' because that was the sort of paper their mum and dad got and they never even thought of questioning whether it was a left-wing or a right-wing paper, let alone whether they should read it. It was only through punk rock that they started to question it. I mean, it's just the little things that happen that change people's lives.

It did make me think. I'd never thought particularly about any social issues, and then you had the Clash, not that their lyrics were particularly deep, but they really got you thinking again about inner-city decay, 'London's Burning' and the town's falling down around them. It's a simple sort of message but it really woke you up.

For those who wanted a deeper philosophy, there was the opportunity in punk to drone on at length about semiology, Jean Genet and Baudelaire

▼ **Poly Styrene, singer with X-Ray Spex, making a forcible point.**

pretty vacant

('When I have inspired universal disgust, then I shall have conquered solitude'). A *Sunday Times* writer who ventured to suggest that the 'deliberate self-denigration' of punks was frightening was answered by 'Maxine – a punk' who smacked her about the head with lines like 'Has she never heard of Kurt Schwitters, Georges Braque, Man Ray? ... We do not reject love and sex. We do reject the fiction-romance teen-dream machine's attempt to brainwash us all into believing that True Love will solve all our problems. No-one with a brain in their head could be deceived by all that schmaltz in magazines, pop songs, or on television, with all its inherent sexism, racism and class stigma.'

But as a rule, punk philosophy was more fun than that.

'Cos there was the Jubilee scene in '77, everyone waving their flags because it was the Royal Jubilee. 'We love the Royal family.' And it was a real big lark at the time, because punk was the complete antithesis of that. We were really going to have a go at it, you know. Having alternative Jubilee parties of anarchy, and the climax of that was obviously 'God Save the Queen' by the Sex Pistols.

When King George V celebrated his Silver Jubilee in 1935, the Communists hung a banner across the processional route and unfurled it as the royal carriage passed below. It read: '25 YEARS OF HUNGER AND WAR'. When his granddaughter celebrated her own Silver Jubilee, the song at number two in the charts (which sold two million copies without even being played on the radio) said:

God save the Queen, a fascist regime
They made you a moron, Potential
H-bomb ...

Two such moments in one century is a generous allowance.

No, there'll never ever be another group like the Sex Pistols, I don't think. They were just completely unique. Their whole attitude seemed to merge with their music. It seemed to be so free. It used to question authority. Just do what you want. It was so brilliant. Yeah, I'd still say 'Never Mind The Bollocks' was one of the best albums ever.

The question of whether Malcolm McLaren 'created' the Sex Pistols has been the subject of a million-pound lawsuit which was resolved in the Pistols' favour. On the other hand, before they met the 'Svengali of Punk' they were a group of seventeen-year-old ex-skinheads who called themselves the Swankers and played sixties pop songs. McLaren added a singer called John Lydon (the name Johnny Rotten was coined by the drummer's mum after she saw the lad's teeth) who wrote vituperative lyrics to the tunes composed by the group's statutory art student, Glen Matlock.

The Sex Pistols' first public appearance at St Martin's College of Art in November 1975 was cut short after ten minutes when the social secretary, who couldn't stand it any more, pulled the plug out; but during that winter the band worked regularly and built up a following of 'Sex' regulars (including Siouxie Sioux who was later to launch a successful recording career on the basis of getting up on stage one night to see what happened). They were banned by the Marquee and the Nashville, but they played frequently at the 100 Club, which in September 1976 attracted 1000 fans to a two-day Punk Festival. On the second day someone threw a glass at the Damned. It missed and blinded a girl in one eye, so then even the 100 Club banned punk. A month later the Sex Pistols signed a £40,000 recording contract with EMI. After the Grundy row, EMI paid them off and A&M signed them up. Within a week their loutish behaviour had so upset the company's management, staff and established artists that A&M too paid them off (£75,000 this time). They ended up with Virgin Records, and 'God Save The Queen' became the fastest-selling single of the year.

People were trying to make money out of it. People like Malcolm McLaren, I mean, he set out to become rich through punk and he achieved it.

The Great Rock'n'Roll Swindle was a film which made its belated appearance long after the Pistols had broken up. It purported to 'expose' the fact that the whole phenomenon had been a cynical con-trick from start to finish. The puckish McLaren appeared with lines like:

pretty vacant

Find yourself a lawyer who has no interest in music, that is purely interested in making money. He's your main asset in developing the highest price and in illustrating to record companies the enormous potential of a band that can't play ... In fact a group that can't play is better than a group that can.

The whole film was about this great swindle, how McLaren claimed he had orchestrated the whole thing just to make a million pounds. We felt, you know, 'Oh dear, we've been had'. But then again, I would say Malcolm McLaren is a bit of a woffler so I wouldn't pay too much attention to what he says, or what anyone says. It certainly was a completely new scene, completely different. I enjoyed it.

Never had I seen, since the days of the Beatles, people queueing up outside a record shop like they did to buy the first Sex Pistols album. But they did that at Virgin Records in Manchester. They were there from 8.30, queueing up outside, waiting for the shop to open to buy this album, and it went straight in at number one. And then all these managing directors and top nobs at big record companies were really embarrassed, because they were all convinced it wasn't going to happen, it wouldn't turn into record sales, it was a live thing. But all these groups, the Pistols, the Clash, the Buzzcocks, all had Top Ten records. They really did rub the bosses' noses in it, you know.

Punk attracted rather more violence than it promoted. In June 1977, various members of the Sex Pistols and their entourage were repeatedly attacked by strangers, some wielding razors, others with iron bars. In July, the Teddy boys took it upon themselves to clean up the streets and the battles of the King's Road began. Like the Bank Holiday clashes of the sixties, they were scuffles that the newspapers turned into riots, partly by over-dramatising them but mainly by publicising them, thereby attracting fresh waves of troublemakers to the following week's encounter. By the third week, gangs of Teds 200-strong were chasing punks through Chelsea to chants of 'We're gonna kill the punks', and the police made thirty-one arrests.

King's Road used to be punk territory at the time. The Teddy boys used to come in and there used to be the lark of having a good old fight or a ruck, just like the mods and rockers. Of course, the papers got hold of that and said it was really sinister, so violent, so terrible, bring back hanging, flogging and National Service. It was just mainly larking about really.

I mean I know people who were actually offered money by photographers to throw bricks at the Teddy boys, but it was arranged with the Teddy boys too, of course, just for the Press.

We used to wind up the Teddy boys, because we used to rush up to them and say 'Have you heard the news?' and they'd go 'What?' and we'd say 'Gene Vincent is DEAD!'

Flirtation with violence is never innocent, however, and punk harboured psychopaths of its own, among them the Sex Pistols' Sid Vicious, who died in New York of a heroin overdose, while awaiting trial for the murder of his twenty-year-old girlfriend.

As 1977 drew to its end, there were signs that the commercial machine had worked out a way of processing punk, adding artificial flavouring and colouring while removing the bits of broken glass. In August, an executive of United Artists Records, who had recently signed up the Stranglers, told the *Evening Standard*:

People in the business are still asking what's new. It's here! This has come from the kids, not from us... But it won't be cool for long because the chic will latch onto it. It will become punk-chic and the kids won't want to know.

It was already happening. In September, a hairdressing salon called 'Mane Line' announced the new 'Pretty Punk' or 'Hedgehog Head' hair-do. In November, the dress designer Zandra Rhodes appeared on the radio talking to Jack de Manio, who introduced her as the 'Queen of Punk'. She was wearing 'a shocking pink jersey tunic' with embroidered holes and chains held in place by beaded safety pins. Similar creations, she said, sold for £200.

*pretty
vacant*

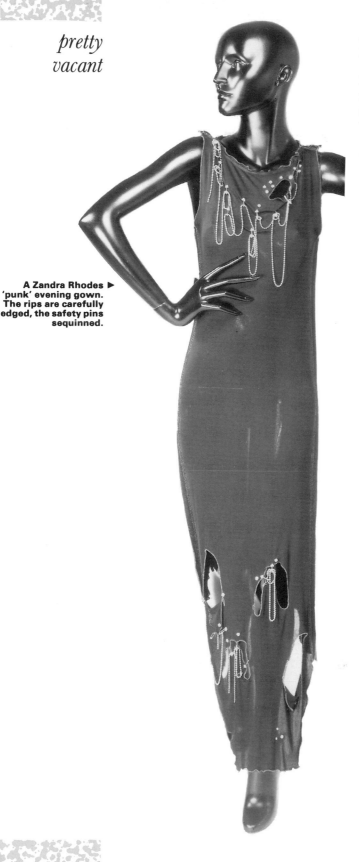

A Zandra Rhodes ▶
'punk' evening gown.
The rips are carefully
edged, the safety pins
sequinned.

Perhaps the last word on 1977 was delivered by Angela Carter in the 29 December edition of *New Society*:

Punk has gone up-market, really up-market, with the most amazing speed, to fuse with the up-market vogue for tacky glitter that has been bubbling under since the early days of the magazine *Andy Warhol's Interview* ... The only difference is, the rich have more money, and are prepared to pay through the nose for gold plastic wrap mini-skirts, plastic raincoats, safety pins (sequinned specially for them) and bondage jackets made up, now, in specifically middle-class fabrics, like good tweed.

The impact of punk ideas on the nation's youth as a whole could be judged by the results of an opinion survey conducted by the Taylor Nelson Group and published in September 1977. Most young people, it concluded, lived at home until they married and got on well with their parents. They wanted an interesting job, a mortgage, a car, two children and an annual package holiday in Spain. They would vote for one of the major political parties and would fight for their country. Three quarters of them 'thought the unemployed could find work if they tried hard enough'.

Dr Elizabeth Nelson, the Group Chairman, commented: 'In the swinging sixties, everyone regarded the under-twenty-fives as the trendsetters in every market you can mention. It was very much a commercial thing, mainly because there were so many of them. They were part of the post-war bulge. But now there is a general moving-away from youth. People have stopped taking so much notice of them and we're just left with a pack of very conventional youngsters.'

In July 1978, *The Sunday Times* took this analysis to its logical conclusion:

'Teenagers' were born in 1942, marketed in 1947, discovered in small flocks in Britain in 1956, cossetted and comforted during the 1960s, began to weaken as the cruel graph of youth unemployment climbed in the 1970s and can now, officially, be pronounced extinct.

oh, what a circus

'It did go rapidly downhill. I mean,
it went beyond the worst it had
ever been before punk happened.
The very élitist club scene,
very expensive clothing . . .
It's just gone back again.'

oh, what a circus

The only sociological essay ever to change the course of teenage history was written by Nik Cohn. Discussing the American youth scene in the mid-seventies, he made the simple point that what everyone thought was youth culture, i.e. being 'alternative', growing your hair and smoking dope, was actually marginal, whereas what everyone thought was marginal, i.e. the commercialised, 'shallow' disco scene, was actually the important bit. Cohn's article, propounding his Perception of the Importance of Disco, was taken up by a film producer who made it into a movie starring John Travolta, and the soundtrack of the film, 'Saturday Night Fever', became the best-selling record of the decade.

Yeah, about 1978 or whatever, there was this great big disco surge. It was John Travolta and 'Saturday Night Fever' and it was really abysmal. We started up the Anti-Disco League and got chucked out of all the cinemas for disrupting the films. But even now I hate discos.

Late-seventies ▶ skinhead style: fascist salute, football scarf, racist sticker on the forehead and an Iron Cross on the anorak-zip.

But it really caught on. I mean, after the film, everybody was going out to dancing lessons and trying this, and there was people who'd never been interested in disco dancing before. So as soon as you heard a Bee Gees record it sparked it off, and there was Macho Man, came onto the dance floor and started dancing.

The men would try and base their image on John Travolta, which was the slightly flared trousers, the three-piece suit with the shirt collar out and a medallion round the neck, or they'd have these shirts with the buttons undone to the waist. They'd be putting their hands in their waistcoat pockets and trying to spin and turn and strutting about and the girls just stood by and watched. They were just posing. It was a real turn-off.

The scene then was just to look cool. You spent most of your time in the toilet, changing clothes. You used to go to the disco with a massive big bag and you had about seven changes of clothes in it and you'd have your towel and your body deodorant to get rid of the smell of sweat, because you'd end up sweating and you'd walk past someone and they'd say 'Oh no,

please!' and then you'd have to go into the toilet and change. So you'd throw off what you'd just had on and put something fresh on, and you'd go on the floor and come back about half an hour later and change again.

The narcissistic escapism of disco represented the opposite approach from punk, but it was a response to the same set of problems. If punk was a primal scream, disco, with its warmth, its heartbeat throb, its darkness, security and freedom from responsibility, was a return to the womb. Black youth felt the same impulse and was drawn to the dance-music culture of 'jazz-funk' which, unlike Rasta, coped with the outside world by ignoring its existence.

Every disco had its bouncers, and their job was to keep out scruffs and troublemakers. Whereas punks, out for the evening, would feel that if there weren't a few troublemakers present they'd come to the wrong place, disco left the lumpen element out in the cold where it grew nastier. The flotsam of punk was caught by a new wave of skinhead aggro and was thrown up again as 'Oi'.

What remained of punk became known as Oi, Oi music, which I couldn't stick at all. I remembered when the National Front had called punks the 'white niggers' and punks were getting smacked about by skinheads, but Oi seemed to unite punks and skinheads. I'm sure there were pockets of philanthropy in the Oi movement, but predominantly it came over as a racist thing, and I couldn't stomach Oi at all.

The punk groups either disbanded or modulated, under the influence of marketing-conscious record company executives, into 'new wave'. This 'acceptable face of punk' wore short hair and an unsmiling face and its records arrived in trendily-designed album sleeves. Its statement to the world amounted to an assertion of its newness. The bands that predated the summer of '76 were dismissed as clapped-out fogies; the newcomers sought to be clean, sharp, relevant, staccato and pure. By the end of the decade, the more talented new wave luminaries, such as the Jam, the Police and Elvis Costello, having lost both their novelty and their 'alternative' status, were fully integrated into the pop establishment. Meanwhile, the Oi bands took punk music in its original guitar-thrashing, four-letter-lyric style and used it to express an inchoate, half-fascist, half-anarchist view of the world. They were against the establishment, but they were against it because it was too soft on 'commies' and blacks, too hard on young unemployed whites like them. The adoption of some of the outward elements of punk, such as bullet-belts and parrot-head hair-cuts, did not disguise the adherents of Oi. Some were ex-punks, some not, but first and foremost they were skinheads.

We became punks because we wanted to associate ourselves with something. We wanted to forget about being bossed about at work all week and just look forward to meeting up with your mates on a Saturday. But when we found out all the punks were middle-class kids from Knightsbridge paying £40 for a pair of bondage strides, we jacked it in and became skinheads.

On 2 July 1981, a Pakistani woman and her three children were killed when their house in Walthamstow was set on fire. The following evening, a concert at the Hambrough Tavern in Southall, featuring the Four Skins, the Last Resort and The Business, was the scene of bitter fighting between skinheads and Asian youths. The Tavern was burned to the ground. This was an extreme example, but there were many more such incidents: where Asians in the early seventies had gone in fear of being beaten up and kicked by skinheads, they now felt justifiably afraid for their lives. In London, in Coventry and elsewhere, Pakistani youths were attacked for no reason and stabbed to death.

I goes into this Chinese chippy. I've got me National Front badge on, and I've got me England badge, and they all look at it and they start jabbering away in Chinese, you know, and I can tell they're calling me, saying 'Oh, look who we've got in', like that. And if you take the piss out of them, they won't serve you and they chuck you out!

I've got 'A.C.A.B.' on my fingers. All Coppers Are Bastards. That's the only tattoo I've got. I can't afford them, they're too dear. I got a bollocking off me Mam for it. She says 'Well, I hope the coppers don't see it when they get you, 'cos they'll give you a good hiding.'

When I was about fourteen I seen it on the television about skinheads and I thought 'Bloody Hell, it must be great to be one of them.' Then when I turned fifteen, I got my first pair of Doc Martens; got the money off my dad and went and had my hair cut. It just kicked off from there. Then I met Swazzy and he got me into the National Front and they told me what it's all about and I agree with it. There's too many blacks coming in, and they're complaining about jobs, right? Five million blacks, right? Three million unemployed. That's like twice the number of whities – that's us, right? – out of work. And we're not rioting. You're black, right? You belong in your own country.

(In 1981, the number of non-white people in Britain was estimated at 2·5 million. 88% of young people, when asked to guess, thought the number was higher than that. 41% of the unskilled working class guessed at a figure of over 10 million.)

141

oh, what a circus

The Anti-Nazi League and its musical offshoot 'Rock Against Racism' took up the challenge of the National Front's drive to recruit working-class youth to the racialist cause. Among the bands who performed free at Rock Against Racism concerts and festivals were those who had suffered at the hands of the skinheads, like the Clash and the British reggae bands, as well as others who were embarrassed by the skinhead element among their own following, like the Specials and Sham 69. It was a paradox of the time that skinheads liked reggae. A sizeable contingent of them joined the 100,000-strong Anti-Nazi League march from Trafalgar Square to Victoria Park in the summer of 1977 because they wanted to hear the black group Steel Pulse. The skinheads who followed the Specials referred to the band, which contained two black musicians, as 'The Specials Plus Two'.

My involvement with Rock Against Racism? I wore the badge. But then everybody wore the badges.

We used to chat with the Rastamen. We got on well with them. Yeah, I went to Hyde Park when they had the 'Rock Against Racism' gig. It was the Clash, Steel Pulse, Sham 69, and when we got there the first fifteen or so rows in front of the main stage were packed solid with National Front skinheads daring anyone to enjoy themselves and speak against racism. They just sort of broke the whole gig up.

▼ A Rock Against Racism concert in Victoria Park . . . an echo of sixties idealism, ten years on.

In Liverpool we had a club called 'Eric's', and there black people and white people came together, because you'd have a punk group supporting a big reggae band from Jamaica. There was a crossover, you know, between the punk and the reggae thing.

The musical links between black and white, forged in the heat of the punk explosion, remained after punk and Rasta went their separate ways. The new meeting point was the mod revival of 1978–9, largely inspired by the film of the Who album 'Quadrophenia', which in turn revived interest in the ska and bluebeat music favoured by the first-generation mods. In London and, significantly, in the 'ghost town' of Coventry (one of the areas hardest hit by unemployment and a town which had seen more than its share of racial violence) new bands appeared wearing 'rude boy' suits and porkpie hats and performing Prince Buster tunes with much wagging of the right index finger. The collective name for Madness, the Specials, Selecter and similar outfits, taken partly from the record label, partly from their anti-racialist stance and partly from their trousers, was Two-Tone.

The appearance of black and white musicians in the same group, which was a novelty in 1979, has become unremarkable in the eighties (although the final barrier will not have been crossed until it is commonplace to see a black lead singer using a white rhythm section). The reggae influence on mainstream pop, from Paul Simon through to the Police and Culture Club, has been even more pervasive.

Infinitely more important than these musical manoeuvrings, however, as an influence on how black and white youths felt about each other and about the wider world, were the outbreaks of inner-city rioting that occurred in Bristol in April 1980 and in London, Liverpool and Manchester at the end of July 1981.

Substantial tomes have since been produced on the causes and consequences of the 'disturbances'. They have been blamed on unemployment, ghetto-isation, insensitive policing, sinister agitators from the 'loony left', the media, and a criminal conspiracy to steal televisions, video-recorders and coffee tables by smashing shop windows while confederates held the police at bay. In

the context of teenage history, what matters is what the young people who fought the police, and those who saw it happening live on television, *thought* it was all about.

In Liverpool, it was definitely the police. They arrested this guy on a bike, they claimed it was stolen and they were going to take him away. There was a mixture of people there, black and white, Indian and Chinese. Everybody said 'You're not taking away the youth', you know, and they wouldn't let them take him away. Next thing, they sent for reinforcements and, without exaggeration, there was at least ten vans down there and a couple of cars, and some of the people, seeing all these police, well a scuffle broke out and the youth that they wanted, he got off, and everybody just stayed and wouldn't let the vans move. And then they turned the engines on and drove at the crowd, and the crowd had to move. And that night, tension was high in the area and any police that they see they just bricked, and it just escalated from there.

It was just black and white people standing together. That is what they were hiding, the fact that just young people were saying 'No, we're not having police harrassment'.

Our children are suffering. They are crying for help. Nobody will listen, nobody wants to take notice. They are making them feel like criminals as soon as they come out on the streets. When will it stop? This is not the right way, but it is the only way you can meet violence. I am a peaceful person, I am, but I am afraid this is the only way you can get action. It should never happen, I regret it.

I've got no time for pigs. The only good pig to me is a dead one.

They rebelled against it in the riots and they haven't achieved anything for themselves. I mean, things have got worse if anything, instead of better. I know it was a run-down place, but they haven't even cleared it up. It's terrible. You know when it happened I phoned up a friend who was there and I said 'Why was there riots?' and he said 'Well, it was all right really', and I said 'Oh come on, why did you do it?' He said 'Well, we wanted people to listen to us. You don't understand, Pat, what it's like living in this area. It's horrible'. And I said 'Yeah, but you should have gone through the right channels'. But the thing is, they had been trying. They had been trying and he said it just wasn't any good.

The oddest post-punk synthesis was the blending of new wave music and disco. The formula took the blank-voiced android singer who never ever smiled and added the synthesised plink-plunks of an intergalactic telephone exchange as backing. Bowie was an influence, having been among the first avant-garde figures to take disco seriously. Another influence was the German band Kraftwerk who on occasion would replace themselves on stage with plastic dummies, switch on the tape-recorder and leave the audience to get on with it. Gary Numan of Tubeway Army, immobile at the microphone in a black shirt and a white face, was alienation personified. Tik and Tok, who wore white boiler-suits decorated with fairy-lights, became popular for their ability to lurch about, swivelling their heads and limbs like robots. Robot dancing spread to the disco, where the dance floor increasingly came to resemble a tray full of clockwork toys. It looked almost as though an incautious jostle on the way to the bar might leave two or three hap-

▼ **Upper Parliament Street, Toxteth, July 1981: the fire-hose vs the half-brick.**

oh, what a circus

less dancers on their backs, clicking and whirring, unable to right themselves.

At the peak of the pyramid of club and disco elitism was one Stephen Harrington from Wales. In 1978, under the alias Steve Strange, he ran 'Bowie Nights' at a gay club in Soho called Billy's. It was his stroke of genius to institute a policy that as few people as possible should be admitted, and that those who were should be rich, famous or friends of his. It was an idea whose time had come. By 1980, Strange was running the Blitz wine bar and disco in Covent Garden, and had got himself into the papers as arbiter of taste to his very own cult, the Blitz Kids.

The *Daily Mirror* proclaimed:

A new youth cult is, according to its bizarre disciples, all set to sweep Britain. They call themselves the Blitz Kids. Their idea of fun is sheer fantasy and almost anything goes . . . THEY DRESS in clothes ranging from crinolines to clown costumes. THEY LISTEN to loud, repetitive electronic music by cult bands. THEY DANCE using a mesmeric mixture of mime and robot movements.

▼ **Steve Strange in an outfit which was admired but not widely imitated.**

Taking with him his one priceless asset, a complete lack of a sense of the ridiculous, Strange moved on to run Club for Heroes, Hell and The Palace. He spent £250 a week on clothes and formed a band called Visage which sold several million LPs. 'If other people laugh at me', he was quoted as saying, 'that's their problem.'

The wider movement which spread rapidly into the provinces, disseminated through television and magazine pictures of bands dressed as characters out of *Robin Hood*, *Rob Roy*, *Treasure Island*, *Gone With The Wind* and *Ben Hur*, was appropriately known as 'new romantic'. As commerce struggled to get a handle on the craze, boiling it down to a basic uniform of frilly shirts and satin knickerbockers, the London style-setters grew ever weirder in their quest for peculiarity. Folk memories of every teenage style up to and including early punk (a whole teenage generation ago) were racked for inspiration. Reporting from the Camden Palace disco in May 1983, the *New Standard* informed its readers:

Hair-styles here command airspace of their own. Clothes are not so much worn as incidentally attached to the body. It's pointless wondering why that girl has coloured her breasts green or why that young man sports fishnets beneath shredded jeans . . .

In other words, the teenagers who went to places like the Palace were, sartorially speaking, on their own. They were required to be unique in the right way (unique in the wrong way wouldn't get them past the door) and there were *no clues*. Such a burdensome state of affairs could not last, however, and by the end of the year it was clear that a particular venue played a particular kind of music for patrons who dressed in a particular sort of way. Seen from outside, the scene was as confusing as ever, but the kids now knew where they were. The Batcave, for example, was pure *Rocky Horror Show*. ('The most important club London has seen since the demise of Blitz . . . a three-way pile-up between a train load of punks, a tanker of eyeliner and an army of Kiss clones' – *Time Out*.) Outside London, the teenagers had been doing their best

to keep up by paying very close attention to 'Top of the Pops' (just as, fifteen years before, the hicks from the sticks had sat with a notebook and pencil to watch 'Ready Steady Go!'). The image which leapt out at them was that of Adam Ant.

Adam and the Ants, a punk band fallen upon hard times, had gone for advice to Malcolm McLaren, who had introduced them to African tribal rhythms and lipgloss. In 1980, Adam emerged in swashbuckling clothes (designed by Vivienne Westwood) with the theory (repeated every time he was interviewed, which was often) that the best way to cope with hard times was to dress like a proud warrior. Just as Bowie's look had changed for every album cover, so Adam Ant worked his way through the Red Indian look, the Regency dandy look, the Prince Charming look ...

To be a new romantic you had to be working and you had to have a lot of money to spend on very, very expensive clothes.

It's the peacock. It's dressing up again, where with punk you really dressed down, you looked like you'd just crawled out of a dustbin, but now you're getting a chance to show off, to put on very extravagant blouses and tie sashes round you and wear voluminous trousers and headbands and make yourself look attractive.

Adam Ant mainly started it all with frilly blouses and pencilling hearts on your forehead and knickerbockers, although that was partly Princess Diana's influence, the knickerbockers. But it was just a gimmick.

The lasting significance of Adam Ant was that he demonstrated to the pop industry the possibility of putting together a complete package – song lyric, video, stage act, dress style – every element of which would reinforce a memorable fantasy in the public mind. For the Prince Charming Christmas Show at Drury Lane Theatre he even, as he put it, 'attacked the nose'. He had the auditorium sprayed with lavender to recreate the smell of an eighteenth-century theatre. The experiment was discontinued after complaints that some of the fans were suffering from hay-fever. Adam Ant was a triumph of marketing.

He helped to return 'image' (the sixties' buzz word which had become a seventies' term of abuse) to its present status as the most important word in the pop vocabulary.

The blatancy with which eighties pop stars cultivated their images, and their readiness to dismiss any suggestion that they might be 'about' anything more profound than an eye-catching appearance wedded to an ear-catching tune, was either refreshing or depressing according to one's expectations of pop music. It would certainly have shocked both the hippies and the punks. It is ironic that punk's best-known gay, Tom Robinson of the Tom Robinson Band, a devout campaigner for left-wing causes including Gay Lib, achieved far less acceptance for that cause among the British public than did cuddly gender-bender Boy George, whose most profound public statement was 'I'm just a show-off'.

Boy George did have his own image, but it was a very different image from Adam and the Ants and very different from punk. The music that went with it wasn't very different from what was around at the time, but he stood out, I think that's what

▼ **Adam Ant, unsure whether this week he's cabin-boy or cowboy.**

oh, what
a circus

*made the difference. And he came at a good
time, because at the time gays were under
a lot of pressure, weren't they? And they
were trying to come forward and make a
point, that, you know 'We are acceptable',
and I think he did a lot for them. I think
he caused a big stir, especially among older
people, and I think that's why younger
people liked him, because he shocked their
parents, and my grandparents were going
'Ooh! Good Heavens above, who's that?'*

New Society made the point explicit:

Culture Club are the most mindlessly
apolitical performers since Muffin
the Mule ... Yet, just by existing in
all his ambiguous glory, Boy George
is sowing seeds of a tolerance that will
probably come to righteous, modest
bloom in, oh, say five years' time ...
when his legions of fans, married to
a mortgage by now, hear a joke about
a queer ... remember how much they
loved him ... and don't laugh.

This is not to say that to be 'mindlessly
apolitical' was necessarily to be an agent
of enlightenment, as the case of heavy
metal neatly demonstrates. The *Guardian* in July 1980 called it 'the phenomenon of the year in British rock'. A survival from the early seventies, when it
had been known as 'heavy rock' or
'downer rock' (associated as it was with
barbiturate abuse), heavy metal
acquired that name from the group The
Heavy Metal Kids (lead singer Gary Hol-
ton, who moved on to acting and thence
to an early death through heroin) who in
turn took it from the writings of William
Burroughs. (No other writer, with the
possible exception of J. R. R. Tolkien,
has christened more rock bands.)
   Heavy metal has been called the
worst form of rock music ever invented,
but it has survived virtually unchanged
for fifteen years, an eternity in rock
terms, and its acolytes never seem to get
any older. Musically it is a riff-based,
guitar-drums-and-yelled-vocals   style,
ranging from brain-numbing twelve-bar
boogie (Status Quo) to melodramatic
post-pomp posturing (Judas Priest)
and always louder than anyone who has
not experienced it can possibly imagine.
Lyrics are aggressively macho, often
expressing intentions which, if enacted,
would attract a charge of indecent
assault at the very least.

Visually, on stage and album cover,
the style tends towards high camp, often
blending Satanism, Nazi chic and
fashions derived from the pornographic
end of the science-fantasy magazine
market. The musicians perform phallic
rituals with their guitars for an audience
which is almost exclusively male, long-
haired and dressed in the metal-freak's
uniform of ratty leather jacket embla-
zoned with the names of favourite
groups (usually in gothic script) and
encrusted with badges, well-worn jeans
(still flared until remarkably recently)
and souvenir T-shirts. At one time, cardboard guitars were sold outside the concerts so that members of the audience
could pose along to the solos.
   The explanation for heavy metal's
enduring appeal may be that it fulfils a
sub-sexual function for the adolescent
male (another term for the music is 'cock
rock'), rather as screaming at pretty-boy
groups affords release to the over-
wrought emotions of the pre-teen
female. It is, however, ironic that the
style began under the name 'progressive'.

The established view of what happened
to teenage culture in the early eighties
is that it fragmented. Martin Walker told
Guardian readers in December 1980:

For once, there is no dominant musical form. They all exist together.
Reggae, funk, new wave, heavy
metal, disco. There's a new magazine
about called *ZG* which has noticed
the phenomenon and describes it
well: 'a mixture of youth cultures
depending on the band playing that
night. It might be punk and skin or
mod and rudie. It's like entering a
living museum of the recent subcultural past.'

The following May, the *Birmingham
Post* set this observation into an economic and political context:

Growing up has never been easy, but
for the eighties teenagers the press-
ures are greater than ever before.
Yesterday's teenagers won most of
their battles for them – sexual
freedom, their own music, clothes
and culture – yet left an additional
legacy of unemployment, economic

depression and world tension. So they can only ape the fashions and pop songs of previous generations or move outrageously towards nihilism ... During the sixties, the youth movement combined to rebel against the adult world. Today youngsters divide very clearly into cults – punk, skinhead, heavy metallers, mod or Ted.

By April 1983 this had become received wisdom. A psychologist told delegates at a London advertising conference that teenagers 'had been left in a backwater'. Musical tastes were 'diverse' and 'anarchic'. There was 'a trend to individual listening boosted by Walkman-type stereo headsets, on which the teenagers can listen to favourite songs, safe in their own private world.'

By October 1983, *Time* magazine was ready to tell the world about 'The Tribes of Britain' which it called 'a complex and curious web of alternative cultures'. *Time* listed punks, skinheads, trendies, Teddy boys, rockabillies, bikers, mods, Sloane Rangers and soccer hooligans.

It seemed a perverse assemblage of stereotypes, but the analysis – that this was 'a generation of alienated youths who have turned to tribalism to give their lives meaning' – was what every 'authority' had been saying for some time.

Having explained that style was an assertion of individualism amid the encircling gloom, most commentators put the dust-covers back on their typewriters and went home. There is more to be said.

First, the very visible cults whose members paraded on the streets and in their specialist nightclubs were not the tip of the iceberg of British youth; they were representative only of themselves. They were more *noticeable* because youth culture, along with the economy, was in recession; just as when the tide goes out it is easier to spot the rocks, wrecks and clumps of seaweed. If 90% of youth (the figure is guesswork) drifts back to dressing from Debenhams and listening to the Top Twenty, the 10% that holds out for an alternative, *any* alternative, is the bit that gets noticed.

Second, all the published lists of 'tribes' (of which there were many, all different) muddled *subcultures* (dress plus music plus life-style) with mere *fashions*. Teenagers themselves do the same thing, of course: a vogue for 'flat-top' hair-styles (shaved at the sides, *en brosse* on top) is seen as having created a whole new 'flat-top' youth culture; a brief revival of music in the style of the late sixties is lumped together with an outbreak of Paisley shirts and suddenly there is a 'new psychedelic movement'; a coterie of middle-class post-punks decides to dress in black and they are 'gothics'.

The third point that the *Time* school

▼ **The Birmingham pop-reggae band UB40 make political points in a tuneful and unpretentious style.**

oh, what a circus

of subcultural theorists tend to overlook is the continuing importance of the class system in British society. The simultaneous existence of – to take two of their 'tribes' – skinheads and Sloane Rangers is hardly evidence that a previously-unified youth culture has now fragmented. Below the level at which the cross-currents of fashion muddy the waters, there are perhaps half a dozen 'life-style' cults, but at bottom there are only three significant groups among British youth in the eighties: the middle class, the working class in work and the working class on the dole.

Secure in the knowledge that their vowel sounds are fine, the children of the middle classes can afford to look scruffy. They will not be confused with the workers, with whom they seldom mix anyway. Deriving their self-esteem from other things, they don't need to belong to lookalike gangs and can afford to cultivate individualism. If they flirt with subcultural style, it is in the spirit of children trying on clothes that they found in a trunk in the attic.

You either look sort of new and sparkling as though you've just stepped out of Benetton, or you look beaten about and scruffy and interesting. Me and my friends just kind of go out of our way to be interesting, unusual and untrendy. We probably fail abysmally but you've got to be something.

It's now considered trendy not to be trendy, with groups like the Smiths, baggy suits, shirts hanging off them, National Health glasses and daffodils in their pockets.

I think some punks can look really nice actually, you know. I mean, black suits some people. I mean, it's quite a sort of flattering fashion if you do it right, the black and threatening look, it can look good. I once dressed up as a punk just to see what people would think of me, you know, for a joke. I sprayed all my hair blue and dressed up in safety pins and leather, and it was really weird, the reactions you got when you were on the bus, because everyone looked terrified of you. I mean you know you're still the same person inside, it's just other people think 'Oh God, she's a punk, she's going to bash me up' sort of thing. So I suppose some

people use it as a kind of way of protecting themselves, to make them feel more threatening. It was a bit worrying, though. We were just sitting in a café, drinking black coffee to keep up the image, and this old lady came across and said 'I must compliment you on your style of dress. There's some punks outside and they haven't tried at all.'

At the bottom end of the social scale, where youth is unemployed or on exploitation wages, style – if it is a consideration at all – is strongly rooted in such subcultures as punk, skinhead or rockabilly (Teds veering towards skinheads in that they prefer white, country-flavoured rock'n'roll and identify with Southern redneck racism. The Confederate flag is a popular emblem.) Occasionally these groups fight each other, as in April 1982 when a punk was stabbed to death by rockabillies at Green Park Underground station, or in April 1984 when skinheads fought rockers at Southend. More usually they coexist in an atmosphere of tolerant indifference.

You can go to the Ritz on a Monday night and there's every type of people there like skinheads, mohicans, flat-tops, and they'll all think differently, they'll all have like different beliefs but they don't talk about it or anything, they just have a laugh, you know? Get drunk or whatever. But there's no fighting. They're all the same sort of people inside, but just like different cults. Everyone's come together but everyone wants to look how they want to look. I mean no-one should be bothered about the way you look. You shouldn't have arguments or fights or hate people as soon as you see them.

It's so boring round our way, you could drop a pin and hear it, so you're just going out nicking, having a laugh. Then if I do get in trouble with the police, it's like a lead weight round my neck, I can't stand it. If I'm going to do anything wrong, I make sure I'm not going to get caught, 'cos I love my Mam. She's always taking tablets and saying 'You're going to be the death of me.' It's probably true but I would never like it to happen.

When I was at school and this punk thing started off, I thought 'That's what I like',

and it was all about not being told what to do. No leaders. Be yourself, right? I'd get this teacher telling me what to do, you know, certain teachers who hated me 'cos I'm better than they are. I thought 'I can't do anything in a school uniform. All I am is a robot with a school uniform on.' So you go to something else. Then people start looking at you and saying 'He's a punk rocker', you know, and I liked that at first. Now I don't. I just like dressing this way. I think the feeling's gone mostly. The feeling's gone out of it, but it's a hard habit to get out of.

Sometimes I feel like 'Why am I doing it?', you know. People are just laughing at me. And I go around with straight people, and they don't laugh at them. They laugh at me and I think 'Sod it', you know? ... Sometimes people don't look at me at all, so then I have to do something different like dye my hair again.

It being easier to think up a new name for an existing pattern of behaviour than to devise a new way of behaving, the punks' pogo-ing became, with very little modification, 'slam dancing', and the rockabillies mutated imperceptibly into 'psychobillies'. The *Daily Mirror*, in June 1985, gave it the usual treatment:

A violent dance craze is sweeping the Midlands. Youngsters who go 'slam dancing' have already caused havoc at dance-halls and caused doctors to worry about the danger involved. The excited boys and girls, some of them as young as fifteen, barge into each other with heads shaking and fists and legs flailing. After hours on the dance floor, the weary dancers can hardly move through exhaustion and their injuries. The fad is linked to 'psychobilly' pop groups.

You've got all the psychobilly music and everything and people go round, you know; dancing and banging into each other. I can see how people can go for it. They're not violent though. You get thrown around a lot and you're flying round the hall, sort of thing, but no-one is trying to hit you. It's just the way they dance. I mean if · someone clonks you over the head – which happens – they say 'Oh, sorry'.

The deepest social division in the early eighties was between those in work and those out of it, and the most insistent subcultural style was the one that marked its exponents as belonging to the ranks of the saved. Variously known as soul boys, crocs, casuals, trendies, top boys (and top girls) and mall girls (though not, apparently, mall boys), it amounted to little more than flaunting expensive clothes and drinking champagne cocktails in glitzy wine bars.

The picture is slightly fuzzed by the understandable wish of those on the wrong side of the great divide to gain admission to the right side, which led to a lot of shop-lifting and the innovative offence of mugging-for-clothes (or 'taxing').

Oh, they're all top boys now. Top boys and top girls, with flares. Flares have come back in very big. You have to have things from Next and Laura Ashley and it's names as well, designer bags and designer shirts and scarves, because you can see that if something's from a certain shop it's going to be distinctive, very tailor-cut and very smart.

Farrahs, Pringles, Lacoste, Tacchini, Fiorucci and things like that. Adidas. The more expensive, that's what people go for. Sometimes they go breaking into shops just to get the money to buy those things. People are doing bad things just to get the money to buy clothes. People say 'If you save you can buy' but they don't understand, it takes years to save that kind of money.

The *New Standard* pointed out in August 1983:

This sort of highly-specialised flash is nothing new. The Teds, mods and even the original skinheads set absolute store by the quality and correctness of what they wore. And it has always been the case that it's the boys, not the girls, who pay the most careful attention to clothes. What seems different today is the total absence of rebelliousness. Even the music they listen to – either chart sounds or smooth jazz-funk – is soft to the ears of parents brought up on the Who or the Small Faces.

oh, what a circus

The British record industry's most successful year was 1978, when it sold eighty-nine million singles and almost as many albums. Five years later the figures were down 17% for singles and 39% for LPs, and the industry had cut its work-force by almost half. This savage retrenchment can only partly be blamed on the declining purchasing power of teenagers (who were also, because of the drop in the birth-rate during the early sixties, becoming fewer). Spending priorities had changed. Clothes were a more pressing consideration, holidays and evenings out in pubs and clubs had become more important, while domestic entertainment was swinging away from the hi-fi in the direction of television, videos and home computers.

I go out with my boyfriend: we go down the pub. I know I'm not supposed to, but I do. Other than that, I think we just stay in and watch telly really. I don't like to miss my programmes – Crossroads, Coronation Street, East Enders ...

A survey in 1980 showed that over half of the nation's younger teenagers watched television for more than four hours a day. The record industry also blamed illegal home taping from pop radio and borrowed records, but whatever the causes of the slump, the effects of it were to make commercial music blander and more remote from teenagers.

The most profitable markets for British 'product' were now overseas. To hit the US and European markets, pop had to be inoffensive, it had to look as well as sound good, and it needed careful selection and production and intensive promotion.

On the home front, in the early years of the 1980s, the biggest-selling performers were those who could appeal to the most affluent section of the market, the upwardly mobile bulge, now in their twenties and early thirties. Dire Straits, Paul Young and Alison Moyet turned out easy-listening rock with a nostalgic sixties flavour and enjoyed the bonus of teenage support as well. They were the compact disc superstars of the G-Plan generation.

In the early seventies, record companies who looked at a new act were thinking in terms of a seven-figure investment to launch it into prominence. When posters appeared with the slogan 'At last the world is ready for Bruce Springsteen', a graffitist added on one of them, 'Or if not, CBS has blown this year's promotion budget'. Punk had briefly overthrown the tyranny of the million-dollar hype. By the early eighties, it was back in position, stronger than ever.

On the marketing front, the expensively-made video 'promo', which had evolved as an alternative to the traditional 'live' (i.e. mimed) performance on 'Top of the Pops', became in effect the product. Now every hit record was a soundtrack, a mere souvenir of the movie.

People are just buying singles for the video and not the song, which I think is a bit stupid. I mean there's nothing wrong with bands appearing live on telly, but then you start getting million pound videos and it gets a bit out of hand. It's a bit ridiculous. I mean, you can get good videos, but they're usually very pretentious as well.

('Million pound videos' is a slight exaggeration, but Michael Jackson's promo for the 'Thriller' album did cost a million dollars.)

For many, the video seemed to be a device by which the brain could be surgically removed from pop music while leaving its pretensions intact and functioning. The teenage press acknowledged the new emphasis on glamour: sales of polysyllabic rock papers like *NME* and *Melody Maker* slumped, while the 'pop glossies' zoomed to unprecedented circulations. Chief among them was (and is) *Smash Hits*, which printed song lyrics and colour pictures of groups and whose approach to the pop scene was more enthusiastic than analytical. Magazine publishers targeted teenage girls in particular, with titles like *Mizz*, *Etcetra* (sic) and *Just Seventeen* who in 1985 described their average reader as 'Tracey from Grantham, who is interested in Simon Le Bon, Duran Duran, helping Ethiopia and what life is like for a policewoman who plays football.'

best years of our lives

'The future seems a bit grim, but you've got to buckle down. You've got to work and see what can come of it. The darkest hour is before the light. Perhaps that light will come when I'm a bit older.'

SCHEME

YOUTH TRAINING

UB40

best years of our lives

In the late summer of 1981, when 600,000 teenagers were on the dole, two young men from Widnes gassed themselves with a pipe connected to a car's exhaust. Their joint suicide note began: 'What have we left to live for, now there is no work for anyone?' The Coroner called it 'a clear result of the economic situation in the country'. Mrs Betty Rathbone, the mother of one of the dead boys, was interviewed for Radio Merseyside. She said:

I noticed a change in my son, Graham, during the last three months. He became very withdrawn and he used to sit in the kitchen with his head in his arms, you know? And I used to ask him, I used to say 'What's wrong, Graham? Why aren't you going out?' He said 'Well there's nowhere to go, Mum. There's no jobs, no money, there's nothing to do. You just walk up and down the street. It's the same every day.' I mean, to me, Graham and Sean ... their lives were just beginning at nineteen years of age. I'll always think of Graham as a flower just beginning to bloom, and it was just snapped off.

▼ **Sunderland town centre: no money, no fun.**

In October 1981, *The Times* warned:

The nub of the problem is that there are almost no jobs at all for the academically unqualified and those best-suited for manual work. The lesson seems to be that if Britain doesn't do something drastic about this very soon, in months rather than years, it will be saddled with an unemployed and unemployable lumpen-proletariat, capable only of causing social problems.

Young people reacted in their different ways to the dwindling of their prospects: some were irrationally optimistic; some refused to entertain the minimum of hope that would allow them even to try. When, in the autumn of 1983, a punk apprentice at Rolls Royce, Bristol, opted to be sacked rather than cut off his superglued hair-spikes ('a danger to workmates') his moral stand, which in many previous generations would have seemed unremarkable, obsessed the media for weeks. Interviewed by David 'Kid' Jensen ('How do you actually get super-glue in your hair?' 'Very carefully'), the punk in question, Peter Mortiboy, insisted that: 'There's a lot more to it than a hair-style, and these things — to me anyway and to a lot of us — are more important than money.'

I do not want a job. Well, I want to work for myself, that's the sort of job. I don't want to work for anyone else and have some old man telling me what to do. I don't want that. I want to tell other people what to do.

If you're intelligent, I think you're much more likely to get a good job. But if you're not and you're in an underprivileged background like Moss Side, I mean it's just awful. The place they live is enough to drive anyone up the wall. I'm surprised they don't all commit suicide. I would.

I'd give an arm and a leg for a good job, you know. 'Cos my Mam's working at this chippy and I don't like her working. She can't stand the woman there and she says to me 'If you get a decent job, I'll tell her to shove the job up her arse.' But it's money coming in the house, innit?

Yeah, there is a problem, but it really can't be helped I don't suppose, at the moment.

I mean, I can't even find a Saturday job. I've looked everywhere. Then I got desperate and went to Woolworths and British Home Stores and they're looking for qualifications!

There's nothing really to get depressed about. I know I say 'Oh, I get depressed', but it's not really depression. It's just being totally pissed off.

The Government adopted a carrot-and-stick approach to the problem. The carrot was a programme of subsidised on-the-job training for school-leavers, known at first as the Youth Opportunities Programme (YOPS) and from 1983 as the Youth Training Scheme (YTS). It offered slightly more money than they would have received on the dole to youngsters who spent a period of months learning 'core skills' (though some trainees wondered what was so skilful about sweeping up and stacking shelves). Fewer places were taken up than were available, and the Government threatened to withdraw unemployment benefit from those who had turned down the offer of a place. They opted instead, however, for abolishing the minimum wage for people under twenty-one, with the aim of allowing them to 'price themselves into work'.

In April 1984, Professor Frank Coffield addressed a conference in Cardiff, the theme of which was 'Stress on Adolescents'. He made the point that most eighteen-year-olds were not politically aware, and therefore blamed themselves rather than the economic situation for their failure to find work. 'They've no idea of the cause of unemployment', he said. 'It doesn't connect with their lives. They end up thinking they should have worked for five O Levels if they have three, or nine if they have seven.'

The difference between dropping out and being dropped is the difference between LSD and cannabis on the one hand and glue and heroin on the other. The problem drugs of the eighties were not the drugs that enhance perception, they were the drugs of oblivion.

The short-term effects of inhaling solvent fumes are dizziness, euphoria and hallucinations. The longer-term effects are addiction, lung damage, heart damage, liver damage, brain dam-

age and boils. The media panic about glue-sniffing peaked during the winter of 1983–4. Deaths attributed to solvent abuse (choking on vomit, suffocation, accidents while intoxicated and burns from ignited vapours) had risen from thirteen in 1980 to sixty-one in 1982. One report estimated that 10% of teenagers were regular glue-sniffers and that one in three children under fourteen had experimented with it. A Cumbrian girl, interviewed on the radio, said in chilling tones of slurred belligerence:

–When you're in the glue you're just in perfect peace, you know.
–What's wrong with normal life?
–Well, because you've got people getting on your nerves and that, and you've got all sorts of problems and things like that.
–And you think glue can get you out of it?
–Well, you're getting out of it for the time you're sniffing it.
–What do your parents think?
–If I knew my parents I'd tell you.

By the end of 1984, the problem appeared to be diminishing due to greater adult vigilance, including that of shopkeepers who now refused to sell glue to young teenagers.

▼ **The person on the right pursues a successful career posing for London souvenir postcards. The one on the left finds this remarkable.**

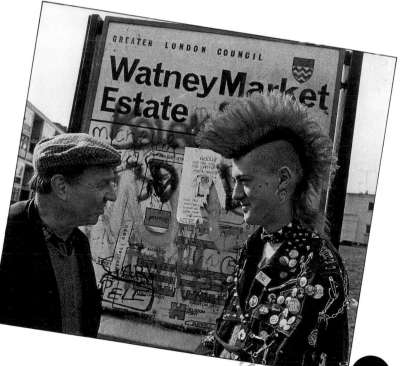

best years of our lives

The more intractable problem was the growing abuse of heroin by teenagers in certain parts of Britain, chiefly council estates with high levels of unemployment. In 1984 it became clear that the number of registered addicts, which had increased from 2441 to 5864 in two years, was only a tiny proportion of the true total of regular heroin users which was now estimated at 50,000. These were not, however, the traditional mainlining junkies. Rather than tinker with the frightening paraphernalia of droppers, syringes and rubber tubes, they preferred to 'Chase the Dragon'.

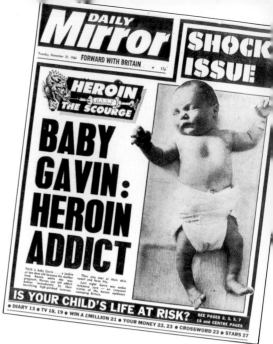

The *Daily Mirror*, in ▶ November 1984, launched an anti-heroin campaign which succeeded in shocking readers. Longer-term success is harder to measure.

This is a bag of smack. It cost me £5. To someone who doesn't know what it is, it just looks like a brown powder wrapped in a piece of paper. What I do is I just tip a certain amount of the smack onto a piece of silver paper, and then hold a match underneath the silver paper so that the smack burns, and I suck up the fumes through a tube.

Taken in this less dramatic way, and available at a price which put it in the same bracket as glue and alcohol, heroin was 'normalised'. The Government responded to public concern with tougher sentences for 'pushers' and a campaign of anti-heroin advertising on posters and television. In Liverpool and elsewhere, those who reckoned the police were ineffective in the matter formed vigilante squads and roughed up suspected heroin dealers. The media hysteria eventually subsided, leaving the problem, as far as anyone could tell, unchanged.

I wouldn't take drugs. At least, I say I wouldn't. I don't think I would. Mind you, I am only fifteen, so there's plenty of time . . .

The most widely-abused drug among teenagers, as among the population at large, continued to be alcohol. Little was said about this, and less done.

With unemployment and drugs at numbers one and two in the teenage problems Top Ten, the sexual behaviour of young people did not give rise to quite so much heavy breathing on the part of the media as had that of their predecessors. The one major battleground was the question of whether doctors should be allowed to supply contraceptive pills to girls under sixteen without their parents' knowledge or approval; a survey in 1984 showed that a third of youngsters had their first experience of sexual intercourse below that age. Caroline Woodruff, General Secretary of the Brook Advisory Centres, was quoted in the *News of the World* as saying 'Young people are pushed into sexual activity by the pressure of the pop music industry, advertising for cosmetics and the prevailing "Everybody does it" attitude.' The issue was fought through the courts, the two sides taking it in turn to claim victory, but in the end it was left up to the doctor in question to make the decision, which was as it had been to begin with.

As far as the over-sixteens are concerned, the heat seems to have gone out of the issue of sexual permissiveness, partly because more of them now feel that mere promiscuity is undesirable, and partly because parents are now less insistent on strict chastity in their daughters. Perhaps surprisingly, permissive attitudes among teenage girls seem to increase as one moves up the social scale. A survey of fifth-form girls in 1985 showed that a third of those at comprehensive schools were opposed to sex before marriage; at grammar schools the figure was 17% and at independent schools a mere 8%. (This may be because sex is most alluring when least available.)

Pop stars, who in their public pronouncements tend to say what they think teenagers want to hear but say it more loudly and crudely than teenagers would care to express it for themselves, are a useful barometer of the public mood. In the mid-eighties, to judge by this measure, we are back to the attitudes of such responsible fifties spokesmen for their generation as Cliff Richard and Adam Faith. In July 1985, the *Mail on Sunday* said:

Nowadays, the pop world is pervaded with puritanism ... Pop stars are the new Moral Majority. If they're not campaigning for the Labour Party, they're raising money for Africa or the unemployed. Your average eighties pop star makes your average bank clerk look raffish and irresponsible.

It quoted Paul Weller of Style Council as saying 'This year I've picked three issues – new trade union rights, CND and International Youth Year.'

The teenagers' response to all this varied from massive approval for the efforts of Bob Geldof and his friends to raise money for starving Africa, to sullen indifference when they were addressed in headmistressy tones by Toyah Wilcox on the Gloria Hunniford show:

I think physical fitness is the greatest form of self-respect you can have, and I think it also keeps your mind in tune, and I always try to preach to young people not to become a slob, and it doesn't take money to run round the block every day, it takes mental discipline ... And nothing is stopping you from learning, and I think the one reason we're on this planet is to learn.

The theme of self-respect for the unemployed through the pursuit of physical fitness (Joy through Strength, to invert an earlier statement of a similar idea) was heavily promoted for a while. It represented an extension down the social scale of the middle-class self-concern which Tom Wolfe had labelled 'the 'Me' generation'. As the bulge-babies struggled – through squash, jogging, aerobics and the purchase of tracksuits – to become less so, there were many latter-day Marie Antoinettes whose message to the poor was 'let them eat muesli'.

In New York, the black culture of 'Hip-hop' – 'rapping' disc-jockeys and break-dancing – was quite consciously promoted as an alternative to gang violence and drugs. When break-dancing spread to Britain, the media made a great fuss of it; kids on the dole were encouraged to waggle their arms about and execute back-flips, rather as prisoners serving life sentences are invited to take up weight-lifting. Nobody ever actually *said* that while these sinuous youths were spinning on their heads on pieces of lino in shopping arcades they were not breaking into other people's houses, but the craze was smiled upon nonetheless.

Pop celebrities of previous generations have remade themselves in the image of the eighties. Mick Jagger is a jogger and Pete Townshend a born-again anti-heroin campaigner. The heavy metal bands have thrown their considerable weight behind the 'Band Aid' and 'Live Aid' famine-relief campaign, producing an all-star single under the collective name 'Hearing Aid'.

And whereas the end undoubtedly justified the means, nobody seemed to think it patronising that the young actors who starred in the children's soap-opera 'Grange Hill' should release a record exhorting teenagers to 'Say No' to drugs. The right of television stars to sermonise to their less privileged contemporaries seems to have become part of Britain's unwritten constitution.

best years of our lives

▼ Break-dancing as a form of busking in Covent Garden.

▲ **Not the first pop star to preach but by far the most effective, Bob Geldof saved lives by offering rock stars the opportunity to show they cared.**

Things like Ethiopia, most people I know just laugh it off and say 'Ha ha, it's not me is it?' I don't think they really want to put their minds to big issues. You know, they'd rather have fun.

I don't like what they're doing with records now, like donating all their money. I mean it's a good cause but they're doing it far too often now. We're just thinking of everyone else and the money's going out and things aren't exactly brilliant for us either. Yeah, we are better off than them. I mean, at least we've got food and clothes on our backs and that. But in a way, they don't know any different.

In 1985, a number of pop stars assembled under the name 'Artists United Against Apartheid', to record a song pledging themselves not to perform in 'Sun City', the South African resort in Bophuthatswana.

Apartheid very definitely makes me hot under the collar, but I don't really do anything about it except go out and buy 'Sun City'. I don't really know what I can do about it, and being a lazy, selfish teenager I don't bother to find out.

Newspapers continue to express surprise at the apathetic conservatism which emerges whenever an opinion poll investigates the attitudes of British youth. An NOP inquiry in 1983 linked this to the growth of pessimism about the state of the world and about their generation's prospects of improving it. The *Daily Mail* reported:

Pessimism among Britain's fifteen to twenty-year-olds about unemployment and their own futures casts a gloomy pall across their young lives. As they look towards the end of the century, increasing numbers of them see the mushroom-clouds of global war blotting out the horizon.

Perhaps it should not have surprised anyone that whereas the optimism of youth in the sixties had found expression in a variety of causes from CND to Save the Whale, the pessimism of the eighties has led to an outbreak of patriotic sentiment and cries of 'I'm All Right Jack'.

A MORI poll during the Falklands conflict found that young people were more in favour of military action against Argentina than were their elders. In the NOP poll of 1983, a majority supported the reintroduction of National Service.

I don't think the bomb will drop in my lifetime. Maybe some time towards the end of the next century. It is inevitable sooner or later.

You have to be worried about it but then again there's no point in worrying yourself over something you don't have that much hold over. It is very frightening, but it doesn't worry me.

I don't actively support CND because I haven't the time. That sounds awful, doesn't it?

I don't feel that there's a great feeling of love and peace amongst young people any more, because everybody has to look after themselves. People don't trust each other like they trusted each other in the late sixties.

There's so much despair among young people. I think there's a lot of despair. They feel 'Well, it's so remote from me that no government is of any concern to

me.' I think they've got a point. I think there's a reason for them not being that basically aware. I don't think it would make that much difference if Mr Kinnock got in tomorrow for five years. I think overall it wouldn't affect my life, it wouldn't affect my family's life. It might affect someone who's homeless, because they're more likely to get a home under Neil Kinnock than Mrs Thatcher. I personally am more supportive of someone like the SDP.

What remains of the 'counter-culture' in the eighties is still largely in the hands and heads of the generations that created it. The hippies still trundle round Wales and the West Country in their old buses, upsetting landowners, visiting free festivals and thanking the Earth Goddess for their supplies of firewood, herbal teas and magic mushrooms. They attract new recruits from among displaced punks and skinheads who have more fun sleeping under tarpaulins than living on council estates, but the leaders are veterans of the Isle of Wight.

Unfortunately, the Women's Movement has remained more of a preoccupation of middle-class graduates in their twenties than a major influence on either the working class in general or on teenage girls in particular. In fact, the force of economic circumstance has actually pushed girls back into the stereotype role from which the Movement set out to free them. According to Professor Coffield, speaking at the 1984 conference quoted earlier, young women were being drawn back into the family, where they worked extremely hard for no pay. 'They disappear from the youth clubs, from the streets, from any interesting activities in which they have been involved.' Another speaker at the conference, Graham Swain, of the National Youth Bureau, said that girls were retreating into early marriage, or, failing that, pregnancy. 'They are not doing it through choice, but through economic necessity, and that's a bad thing. It's the only way they are finding a purpose and identity in adult life.'

There is still idealism among the young and it takes many forms, from militant vegetarianism to attending concerts in support of the Labour Party, but it is minimal by comparison with support for CND in the early sixties or even the Anti-Nazi League in the late seventies.

The significant thing is that Trafalgar Square is not regularly crammed with angry, unemployed teenagers demanding a change of government; inner-city riots are not regular occurrences; the very word 'demo' has a quaint, old-fashioned ring to it. As a group, teenagers do not feel powerful.

As Tony Tyler, ex-Deputy Editor of *New Musical Express*, puts it:

I think one of the things to lament, perhaps, about the teen boom of the fifties through the seventies is that it force-fed a couple of generations with false expectations. It made them seem to themselves more important than they really are. I don't mean that in any nasty way. They're not very important. What can teenagers do? Not very much. What can teenagers know? Not very much. They might have tons of charm and potential, and that's really where the interest in teenagers lies, it's in their potential. That's what's sad about teenagers out of work today: they're not getting a chance to fulfil that potential. I don't know what the answer is.

It's certainly true that, problems though there are today, it was just as bad in another way in the fifties and sixties when they were over-indulged to the point of crass stupidity. A great deal of the angst that kids have today is because they know the respect and adulation that their elder brothers and sisters got – or even their parents, if they've got young parents – and it seems unfair to them that they don't get the same. And I quite understand how they feel. But the truth is that it was unfair to give their parents and their older brothers that kind of treatment. They didn't deserve it. They were only kids. But they were a market and it was essentially a market force. And I'm afraid when you take away the market, you take away the interest. That's why it's finding its own level again. It's rather sad.

Tyler's analysis makes sense as a description of what has happened to the British teenager, but it paints the cloud and leaves out the silver lining. When one looks back over forty years of teenage history, one observation achieves the force of obvious truth: it is that youth culture – fashion, music and philosophy evolved by teenagers for themselves –

has been most alive and creative during the periods when society at large has taken least notice of it. This was true of the rock'n'roll craze before it was taken up by Tin Pan Alley, of Merseybeat before the Beatles became megastars, of mods before Clacton, of hippies before the Flower Pot Men and of punk before Zandra Rhodes invented the sequinned safety pin.

The longer the cork stays in the bottle, the stronger becomes the brew. Part of the problem for youth culture in the seventies and eighties was the determination of record company A & R men, rock journalists, fashion buyers and television producers to sniff, sample, label and decant the 'Next Big Thing' before it had had a chance to ferment. To vary the metaphor, every time teenagers picked up a new toy it was snatched from their hands, polished, mass-produced and sold back to them at a profit.

'It wasn't us', said the men of commerce. 'It came from the streets.'

In the spring of 1986, Bruce Mitchell, who handles the lighting for several of the Manchester clubs that promote live music, said: 'The Next Big Thing? There is no Next Big Thing because there are too many next little things, but more kids are getting together and starting bands than ever before, they're all playing different kinds of music, they're all open to what one another are doing and they're having a wonderful time.'

When something radically new emerges from this creative stew, my wish for it is that it may be a long time before anyone over twenty-five finds out about it.

If you're sixteen now, I mean, it can't be all gloom. There must be some optimism, just from the fact of being sixteen.

**Endlessly recycled ▶
and intellectualised,
youth culture relies
for its originality on
the fact that today's
kids aren't interested
in yesterday. Biff
makes the point...**

acknowledgements

BIFF PRODUCTS page 158
CAMERA PRESS page 100
CBS page 145
ROBERT CRUMB page 116
DECCA INTERNATIONAL page 46
ROBERT ELLIS page 115 top
EMI RECORDS pages 72, 96
SALLY AND RICHARD GREENHILL
pages 142, 152, 153, 155
HULTON PICTURE LIBRARY pages 11
top, 12–26 top, 30, 31, 34, 36, 38, 39, 47,
48 top, 49, 56, 63–67, 75, 79, 81 bottom,
99, 102, 109 bottom, 112, 113, 117, 118,
123 bottom, 124–129, 140
JAY KINNEY page 32
KOBAL COLLECTION pages 28, 76, 81
top left, 82 top, 83 bottom, 85 bottom,
86 top, 88, 89
LONDON FEATURES INTERNATIONAL
pages 33, 115 bottom
NETWORK/JOHN STURROCK page 143
NEW ENGLISH LIBRARY page 109 top
PHOTO SOURCE pages 11 bottom, 37
bottom, 71
POLYDOR page 95 top
POPPERFOTO pages 40, 97
PRESS ASSOCIATION pages 29, 52, 59
REX FEATURES LTD pages 53, 57, 58,
78, 81 top right, 82 bottom right, 83 top,
84 top, 84 bottom right, 85 top, 86
bottom, 87, 90–94, 95 bottom, 104, 105,
133, 144, 147, 156
SKR page 107
MIKE STOLLER COLLECTION page 26
bottom
SYNDICATION INTERNATIONAL page
154
JOHN TOPHAM PICTURE LIBRARY
page 48 bottom
TRINIFOLD LTD page 82 bottom left
UPPA page 123 top
V & A MUSEUM, LONDON page 138
V & A THEATRE MUSEUM page 45
VIRGIN RECORDS pages 131, 135